CELEBRATE CHRISTMAS

by

Kathy J. Jones

illustrated by Vanessa Filkins

Cover by Dan Grossmann

Shining Star Publications, Copyright © 1985
A Division of Good Apple, Inc.

ISBN No. 0-86653-279-X

Standardized Subject Code TA ac

Printing No. 98765432

Shining Star Publications
A Division of Good Apple, Inc.
Box 299
Carthage, IL 62321-0299

Unless otherwise indicated, the King James version of the Bible was used in preparing the activities in this book.

A WORD TO PARENTS & TEACHERS

Celebrate Christmas is a book designed to help you and your children celebrate the entire Christmas season with more fun, more laughter, more love and, hopefully, with more meaning.

This book is filled with recipes, crafts, poetry, games, puzzles, original songs, and more to help center our Christmas thoughts on the birth of our Savior and all the events surrounding that most blessed moment in history. Virtually every activity is centered around the Scriptures to help us all keep Christ in our Christmas. In our commercial-oriented world, this is often difficult to do.

The culminating activity is a Christmas musical designed for young children that includes many of the thirteen original songs presented in this book. Opportunities for making props and costumes to be used in your dramatic presentation are included along with recipes for your cast party refreshments!

This work is divided into twelve sections including the Christmas Potpourri section and *Night of Nights* musical at the end. Each of the other sections centers on a single aspect of the birth of Jesus Christ and the events leading up to and following the first Christmas Eve. As a teacher or parent, you may choose to work through activities as presented or skip around from section to section selecting a variety of activities in which your children may participate.

Any way you choose to use it, *Celebrate Christmas* is sure to help make Jesus the center of your Christmas celebration while preserving all the fun and magic of the season for your children to enjoy as well. Merry Christmas to all.

TABLE OF CONTENTS

SONGS

Shining Star Publications, Copyright © 1985, A division of Good Apple, Inc.

DECEMBER DELIGHTS

1 Use a Christmas symbol to make a dot-to-dot picture.	**2** Make a messenger angel for your door. See page 17.	**3** Solve the camel maze found on page 75. Then make up your own camel maze for a friend.	**4** Play the blindfold game found on page 29.	**5** Fold some stars. Directions are found on page 48.	**6** Illustrate Luke 2:8.	**7** Look at the stars. Imagine how the shepherds felt when they saw a new star in the sky.
8 Write your own Christmas song about angels. Fit it to a familiar Christmas tune. Sing it for your mother.	**9** Make your own wise man crown. Directions and pattern are found on pages 77-78.	**10** Make a shepherd puppet found on page 35.	**11** Weave a Christmas place mat for each person who will have Christmas dinner with you. See page 26.	**12** Make a star mosaic. Directions are found on page 45.	**13** Call an older person and wish him a happy holiday.	**14** Design your own Christmas greeting card. Some hints are found on page 38.
15 See if you can walk like a camel.	**16** Make a heavenly recipe found on page 19.	**17** Read Matthew 1 carefully.	**18** Make some gift-wrap boxes. Directions are found on page 76.	**19** Make a roller box story about the wise men. Directions are found on page 71.	**20** Make nativity napkin rings. Directions are found on page 62.	**21** Make a list of gifts you would like to give Jesus.
22 Make a Christmas bell. See page 20.	**23** Make flannel board characters and tell the Christmas story.	**24** Act out the journey to Bethlehem.	**25**	**26** Go on a bell search. See page 22.	**27** Make a list of things you like best about your dad.	**28** Pantomime the wise men going to see Baby Jesus. Directions are on page 69.
29 Search the book of Genesis to discover the family tree of Jesus.	**30** Make your own tambourine. See page 24.	**31** Form a joy band and march around with some friends singing.				

Shining Star Publications, Copyright © 1985, A division of Good Apple, Inc.

4

MARY AND JOSEPH

"And Joseph also went up from Galilee, out of the city . . . . To be taxed with Mary his espoused wife, being great with child."
Luke 2:4,5

Mary and Joseph are perhaps the most famous parents in all of history. Celebrating Christmas would not be complete without remembering their special story, their journey to Bethlehem, their angelic visitors.

In the pages that follow, discover just how important they were to God, to Jesus, and to all of us.

To discover why Joseph and Mary had to journey from their home in Nazareth to the town of Bethlehem with Mary just about to have a baby, circle the hidden words in the rows of letters below. The first two words are circled for you. Look up the verses in Luke 2 and put the verse numbers in the blanks.

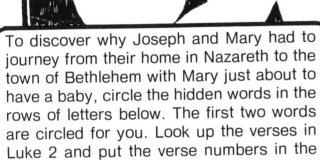

ANDYITPCAMEQHTOXPASS
CINZBTHOSENEDAYSRHNU
THATWTHERETWENTMOUTD
QAPDECREECSFROMGBXUA
CAESARJKOAUGUSTUSMBK
DHJTHATUALLNTTHEAOPZ
WORLDBSHOULDKPLBEWYC
VBTAXEDMSQANDTJOSEPH
ALSOPKWENTTMWUNTOAEK
MTHEKICITYTOFLBDAVID
WIWHICHOVISJCALLEDNL
JBETHLEHEMBKUAZQHJMP
NCRSBECAUSEYVHEUALBD
SHWASUABOFCJRPNTHEHY
WPBSIHOUSEQQANDVREEH
FLINEAGEUOFMDAVIDNQF

LUKE 2: _____, _____

(Answer is found on page 144.)

A LONG, DARK ROAD

Words and Music by Kathy Jones

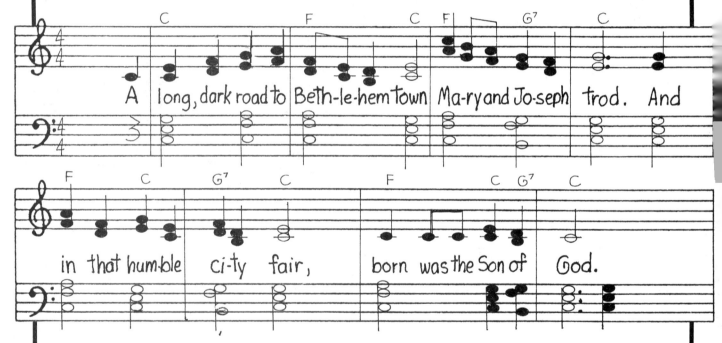

A long, dark road to Beth-le-hem town Ma-ry and Jo-seph trod. And
in that hum-ble ci-ty fair, born was the Son of God.

Verse 2

A long, dark road to Bethlehem town
Lighted by stars above
Did show the shepherds where to find
God's greatest gift of love.

Verse 3

A long, dark road to Bethlehem town
Leading the wise men brave
To Baby Jesus whom God sent
A dying world to save.

"A LONG, DARK ROAD" ACTIVITIES

GETTING READY

Prepare a list of foods and other supplies Mary would have needed to get ready for the trip.

Write a prayer she may have prayed before she left on the long, dark journey.

Pretend you are Mary and traveling to Bethlehem. Write a postcard to your cousin Elisabeth telling her of your travels.

USE A MAP

Get a map of the Holy Land. You might find one in the back of your Bible. Estimate how many miles it is from Nazareth to Bethlehem. Trace a path on the map that shows how Joseph and Mary may have traveled on their journey.

JOSEPH'S JOURNAL

Write a make-believe journal of the trip, as Joseph might have recorded it. List the places through which Joseph and Mary passed. Draw a map to go along with your journal.

MARY'S DIARY

Use the map and trip you planned in Joseph's Journal to write Mary's diary. Include entries in Mary's diary for each day of the trip. Don't forget to write about the night Jesus was born and the days that followed.

A CHRISTMAS HELPER

Connect the dots beginning with number 1 and continuing to number 71. Find out who was Joseph and Mary's special helper on their way to Bethlehem.

I WONDER

Words and Music by Kathy Jones

9

"I WONDER" ACTIVITIES

I WONDER HOW THEY FELT

Lots of events in the Bible cause us to wonder how the people involved must have felt at the time of these important occurrences. Write another "I Wonder" song or poem about the person or people in your favorite Bible stories. Some suggestions:

I wonder how David felt when he saw Goliath.
I wonder how Joseph felt when he was sold into Egypt.
I wonder how Moses felt when he parted the Red Sea.
I wonder how Jesus felt when Peter denied Him.
I wonder how Jesus felt when Judas betrayed Him.
I wonder how Mary felt when Baby Jesus was born.
I wonder how Paul felt when he no longer could see.

FEELINGS OF CHRISTMAS

We have so many special feelings at Christmastime. There are many ways to express them. Try some of these:

1. Decorate a styrofoam or cardboard tree with ribbons. Before tying each ribbon into a bow, write a feeling on each one with a felt tip marker. Each ribbon should have a different feeling of Christmas. Samples: I feel happy. I feel like singing. I feel generous.

2. Write a letter to someone telling him how you feel about Christmas: the sights, the sounds, the smells.

3. Start a Christmas diary or journal! Two weeks before Christmas, write down the events of each day and how you feel about them. Emphasize the sights and sounds of Christmas!

4. Do the same thing with an ART DIARY. Express your feelings about Christmas through drawing, painting, mosaic—any art form or craft.

POINT OF VIEW

Everything that happens can be told from a different point of view: the way you see it, the way I see it, the way someone else sees it.

Write the first Christmas story from Mary's point of view. How did she feel when the shepherds came, when the wise men came, when Baby Jesus was born? Then write the story again from Joseph's point of view. Can you think of some other ways to write the Christmas story that would be a little different, that would show a different point of view?

JOURNEY TO BETHLEHEM

DRAMATIC PLAY: Have the children act out the journey to Bethlehem. Joseph should take great care with Mary, who is about to have a baby. He should show her great courtesy, respect and concern. Have students think about what Joseph would pack on his donkey, what he and Mary would both need. Mary should show great love and gratitude for all that Joseph does. Do not write out what each player will say. Have the children think about it first, then act it out naturally.

Simple costumes (robes, shawls or scarves for headdresses) will add to your drama. Have students take turns playing the two roles of Mary and Joseph to see how different children act out the journey. Remember: have the children make up all the lines as they go along.

OH STARRY NIGHT

OBJECTIVE: To create a beautiful mural to remind everyone of that wonderful night when Jesus was born.

MATERIALS: Black paper for the background, enlarged picture of Mary, Joseph, Baby Jesus and donkey, several boxes of large silver stars and colored chalk.

PROCEDURE: Begin by covering the bulletin board with black paper. Use a transparency of the picture of Mary and Joseph and an overhead projector to get the picture the size you need. Use a light pencil line to draw the picture so that it covers most of the center of the board. Attach the title at the top of the board. Older children should complete this board by coloring the picture using the colored chalk. Complete the board by attaching large silver stars to the background to represent the night sky.

Fold

Fold

Fold

Fold

Fold

Fold

Fold

Fold

Fold

Fold

SNIP-AND-FOLD NATIVITY SCENE
Glue the above picture to heavy paper. Cut along the dash lines, fold along the dotted lines and you have a pop-up nativity scene.

WHO WAS THIS MAN JOSEPH?
by Kathy J. Jones

"WHO WAS THIS MAN JOSEPH?" ACTIVITIES

GENEALOGICAL JOURNEY

Joseph was a very important man in the Scriptures. He was so important that one of the Gospel writers felt it was necessary to trace his lineage all the way back to Abraham. Why do you think he did that? Look up the word *genealogy* in the dictionary. Then look up Joseph's genealogy in Matthew 1. Make a family tree or chart showing the lineage of this great man, Joseph, all the way back to Abraham.

*BONUS CHALLENGE: Search through Genesis to discover the lineage of Abraham and extend Joseph's line on your tree or chart all the way back to Adam!

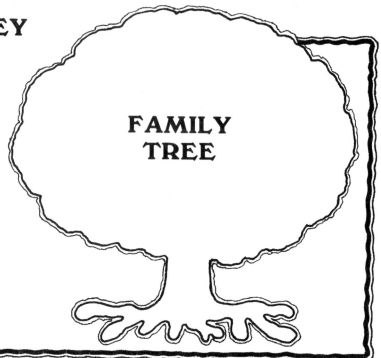

FAMILY TREE

JOSEPH'S PREDICAMENT

Read Matthew 1 carefully. Write out the story of Joseph and the angel Gabriel in the form of a play or short dramatization. Include his courtship with Mary and how heartbroken Joseph must have been when it was discovered Mary was with child. Emphasize his conversation with the angel Gabriel. Consider different ways Joseph may have reacted to the news the angel brought him.

ANGELIC VOICES

In the chorus of the song, a short descant is suggested on the word *Bethlehem.* If someone in your family or class reads music fairly well, have him or her fill in some more high notes on the last line of the song so that the descant can be carried out to the end of the song. One or several people with high voices singing these notes will have the effect of angelic voices echoing the news of the heavenly events taking place in the song. Make sure you harmonize!

JOSEPH, THE FATHER

Try to imagine what kind of father Joseph must have been to the infant Jesus as He grew through boyhood. God must have had a good deal of trust in this man to assign him such a great responsibility. Make a list of special fatherly qualities a man would have to have to be the guardian of "God's only Son." Then, remembering that Jesus had other brothers and sisters, make a Father's Day card to this very special father as if you were one of those brothers or sisters who lived long ago. Perhaps you could write a short poem about your "pretend" father to include in your card.

BUSY ANGELS

The angel Gabriel paid other visits during this sacred moment in history. Search through the four Gospels and record all the times when an angel visited the earth in regard to the life of Christ. There are quite a few! Chart these occurrences below.

ANGELIC VISIT	REASON FOR VISIT	SCRIPTURAL REFERENCE

NIGHT OF NIGHTS

There must have been many star-filled nights on the road to Bethlehem. I wonder what Joseph dreamed about as he went to sleep each night on their journey leading up to that "night of nights." Write about what one of Joseph's dreams may have been and then paint or draw a picture to illustrate his dream.

Shining Star Publications, Copyright © 1985, A division of Good Apple, Inc.

RECIPES FOR THE ROAD

We do not know what kind of food Mary prepared for the journey. We can only guess. Perhaps she took dried fruit, bread and hard cheese. What foods were produced in this area at the time of Christ's birth?

FRUIT & NUT CARAMELS

Place 1 cup raisins and 1 cup chopped nuts in buttered pan. Combine ¾ cup butter and 1 cup brown sugar in saucepan; cook and stir to hard ball stage (254⁰). Pour over raisins. Top with coconut. When the candy cools, cut in squares.

CRUNCHY MUNCHY

1 cup granola cereal
1 cup chopped nuts
1 cup raisins
½ cup coconut
½ cup banana chips

Optional:
½ cup chocolate chips
½ cup miniature marshmallows
½ cup chopped dried pineapple

Stir together and place in a large bowl to serve.

CRANBERRY AND NUT BREAD

2 cups flour
¾ cup sugar
4 teaspoons baking powder
½ teaspoon salt
2 beaten eggs
1 cup milk
3 tablespoons oil

½ cup diced candied citron
½ cup raisins
½ cup chopped nuts
½ cup cranberries

Sift together flour, sugar, baking powder, and salt. Combine eggs, milk and salad oil; add to flour mixture, beating well about ½ minute. Stir in fruits, cranberries, raisins and nuts. Turn into greased loaf pans. Bake at 350⁰ about one hour.

ANGELS, BELLS AND DREAMS

''And the angel came in unto her, and said, Hail, thou that art highly favoured, the Lord is with thee: blessed art thou among women.''   Luke 1:28

From the announcement of the birth of John the Baptist, Christ's cousin and forerunner, to Joseph's warning and flight into Egypt, the Christmas story is filled with angels and dreams from heaven like no other story in the Bible . . . another reason that makes celebrating Christmas so special.

MESSENGER ANGEL FOR YOUR DOOR
(Luke 1-2)

Here is an angel that is sure to brighten any door this holiday! You will need: a roll of Christmas gift wrap, two 9'' paper plates, a roll of gold ribbon, chenille stem, crayons, glue, scissors and tape.

Cut the gift wrap in a large triangle for the dress. Cut two smaller triangles for arms and attach to dress. Draw a face on the paper plate. Cut strips of ribbon, curl it and glue on as hair. If you want a halo on your angel, attach the chenille stem to the angel's head with tape. Attach the head to the body with tape. If you want wings on your angel, cut the other paper plate in half and attach one-half behind each shoulder. Glue the ribbon on the dress as shown. You can also cut features for the face from ribbon or paper and glue them on. Use your imagination! Attach your angel to the door with tape.

STAINED-GLASS ANGEL

Color the stained-glass window below with the correct color for each number listed. See a beautiful angel appear before your eyes!

1 = red
2 = blue
3 = yellow

4 = green
5 = purple

All unnumbered sections should be left white.

ANGEL CAKE SUPREME

1 cup sifted cake flour
1 ¼ cups sifted confectioners' sugar
1 ½ teaspoons cream of tartar
1 ½ cups (12) egg whites
¼ teaspoon almond extract
¼ teaspoon salt
1 ½ teaspoons vanilla
1 cup granulated sugar

Sift flour with confectioners' sugar 3 times. Beat egg whites with cream of tartar, salt, vanilla, and almond extract till stiff enough to hold up soft peaks but still moist and glossy. Beat in the granulated sugar, 2 tablespoons at a time, continuing to beat until meringue holds stiff peaks. Sift about ¼ of flour mixture over whites; fold in lightly with down-up-and-over motion, turning bowl. Fold in remaining flour by fourths. Bake in an ungreased 10-inch tube pan in moderate oven (375º) about 30 minutes or till done. Invert pan, cool thoroughly.

Serving suggestion: Spoon strawberries over cake; add an avalanche of whipped cream.

ANGEL KISS COOKIES

½ c. softened butter	1 tsp. vanilla
½ c. peanut butter	¼ tsp. salt
¾ c. packed br. sugar	1 ¾ c. flour
¼ c. sugar	1 tsp. baking soda
1 egg	3 tbs. sugar

48 chocolate kisses

Beat first 7 ingredients until light and fluffy.

Add flour and soda; thoroughly blend.
Shape into 48 balls. Roll balls in 3 tbs. of sugar. Place 2'' apart on ungreased cookie sheet.

Bake 8-10 min. at 375º. Immediately top each cookie with a kiss, carefully pressing down firmly. Makes 48.

HERALD ANGELS—JOY BRINGERS, JOY MAKERS

The herald angels of the first Christmas brought news of the Christ Child. They also brought the FIRST REAL CHRISTMAS CELEBRATION. A multitude of heavenly hosts made beautiful heavenly music on that first Christmas night. Ever since, Christmas music, especially from joyous bells, helps us celebrate the joy of the Christmas season.

BELL MAKERS, BELL RINGERS

Find plastic bottles with long, fluted necks and wide bases (large vinegar bottles, salad oil bottles, some soft drink bottles). Ahead of time, carefully cut off bottle bottoms. Have the children suspend a string through the neck opening and tape it to the outside. Tie a nut or bolt to the other end to form the bell clapper. Wrap crushed foil over the top of the bottle's neck. Then decorate the "bells" with glue, glitter, sequins, layers of tissue paper and/or poster paint.

JOY MATCH-UP

Bells certainly make us happy. List all the things that make you especially happy at Christmas (bells, presents, candy canes, etc.). Then list all the things that happened at Jesus' birth in one or two words (shepherds, wise men, etc.). Now can you match the Christmas symbol that you love with its original event? See how many you can come up with.

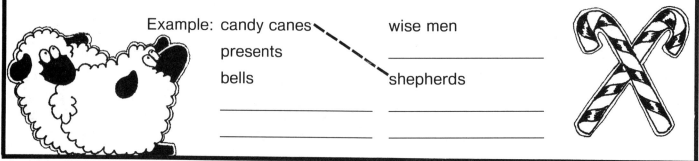

Example: candy canes   wise men

presents   _____

bells   shepherds

_____   _____

_____   _____

LET THE BELLS RING OUT
Words and Music by Kathy Jones

EXTRA! EXTRA! HEAR ALL ABOUT IT

Lots of news is mentioned in the song "Let the Bells Ring Out." Go over the phrases that mention news. Have the class collaborate on the writing of a simple miniplay or skit suggesting various things the shepherds and angels might have said to spread the good news that first Christmas. Then devise some simple costumes, memorize lines, and act out a newsworthy event.

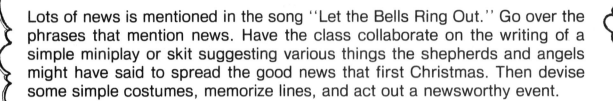

BELL SEARCH

Just what do bells signify at Christmastime? Challenge your class or your family to go on a "bell search" at their public or school library. Have them find out as much as they can about bells, especially in connection with the Christmas season. Then the researchers should report back to home or class with their findings.

GROUP SING

Practice the song "Let the Bells Ring Out" as a group for several weeks until it is memorized. Arrange for a time to perform. Have two class members play "bells" as background accompaniment. Use at least the A and F notes and others as shown in the first two measures that introduce the song. The presentation would be especially effective if boys and girls could dress as shepherds and angels.

MAKE A JOYFUL NOISE UNTO THE LORD

Words and Music by Kathy Jones

"MAKE A JOYFUL NOISE" ACTIVITIES

SOUND SEEKERS

There are joyful noises all around us. God's creations are full of them! Have the children draw pictures with birds, bees, a waterfall, trees, children, etc. Encourage the children to include as many things as they can think of that make joyful noises. Then discuss or have them list the sound that each of the things makes. Examples: water rushing, children laughing.

—TAMBOURINES—

For this activity, you will need a 6-inch or 8-inch diameter metal or plastic ring, which is available through wholesale craft supply stores.

Tie one or more bells on the ring with a long purple ribbon, leaving tie ends long.

SONGS OF THE HEART

Make a grab bag of favorite Christmas songs. Have everyone put the name of his/her favorite song or hymn on a card and place the cards all in a bag or similar container. Each week, select one or two cards and let the contributors be the song leaders. Sing the songs from your heart.

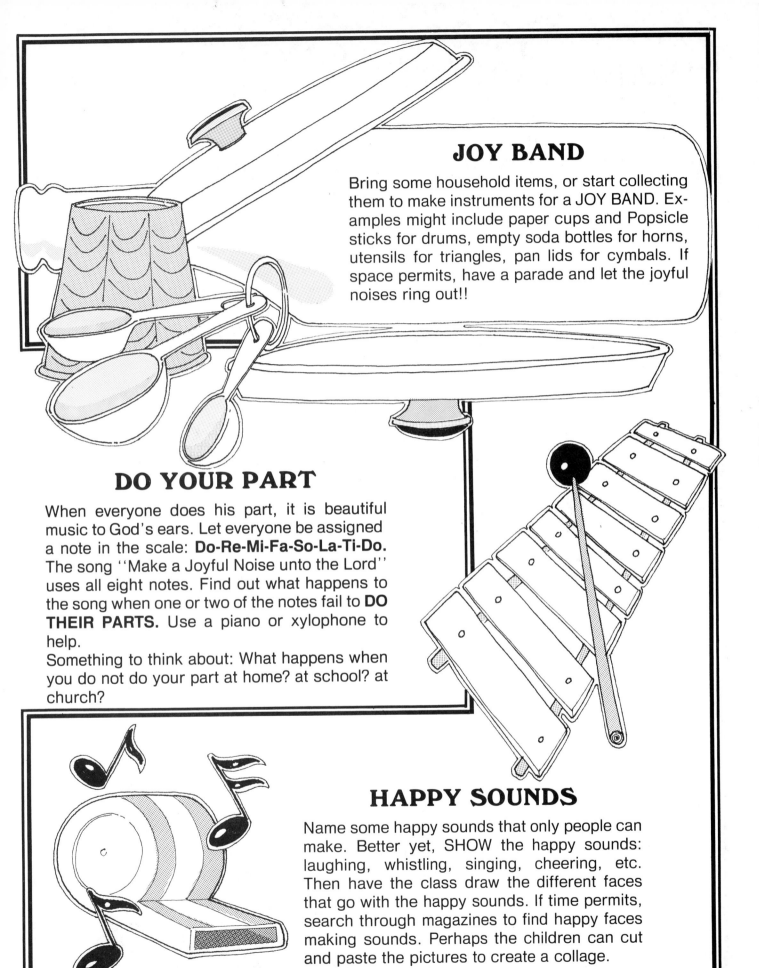

JOY BAND

Bring some household items, or start collecting them to make instruments for a JOY BAND. Examples might include paper cups and Popsicle sticks for drums, empty soda bottles for horns, utensils for triangles, pan lids for cymbals. If space permits, have a parade and let the joyful noises ring out!!

DO YOUR PART

When everyone does his part, it is beautiful music to God's ears. Let everyone be assigned a note in the scale: **Do-Re-Mi-Fa-So-La-Ti-Do.** The song "Make a Joyful Noise unto the Lord" uses all eight notes. Find out what happens to the song when one or two of the notes fail to **DO THEIR PARTS.** Use a piano or xylophone to help.

Something to think about: What happens when you do not do your part at home? at school? at church?

HAPPY SOUNDS

Name some happy sounds that only people can make. Better yet, SHOW the happy sounds: laughing, whistling, singing, cheering, etc. Then have the class draw the different faces that go with the happy sounds. If time permits, search through magazines to find happy faces making sounds. Perhaps the children can cut and paste the pictures to create a collage.

DREAM WEAVER

WEAVE A CHRISTMAS PLACE MAT . . .

Cut 9 strips of green paper, 12'' by 1''.

Cut 12 strips of red paper, 9'' by 1''.

Lay out the green strips lengthwise on a table. Beginning at the left, carefully weave the red strips over and under the 9 strips of green. Start the first one OVER the green, start the second strip UNDER, and so on.

On a white piece of paper, 9'' by 12'', draw a picture in crayon or water colors of one of the DREAMS talked about in the first 2 chapters of Luke or in Matthew 2. Glue or paste your woven mat to the back of your picture.

Now you have a REVERSIBLE PLACE MAT for celebrating your Christmas feast!

RIDDLE RACE

RACE to find the correct letter in each of the Scriptures listed below. As you find the letter, place it in the correct blank to discover the answer to this riddle:

My son came first;
My son left first;
My son prepared His way.
An angel told me of his birth.
I was silent 'til that day.

___ ___ ___ ___ ___ ___ ___ ___ ___
9   4   8   3   6   5   7   1   2

1. Luke 2:13   fourth word, second letter
2. Luke 2:14   sixth word, sixth letter
3. Luke 1:6   fifth word, fourth letter
4. Matt. 1:2   first word, first letter
5. Matt. 2:2   seventh word, third letter
6. Luke 2:2   sixth word, second letter
7. Matt. 1:1   fifth word, eighth letter
8. Luke 2:11   tenth word, first letter
9. Luke 1:67   fourth word, first letter

CHALLENGE RIDDLE:

I am that son;
I was His cousin;
Our births were both foretold.
I leapt for joy when Mary came,
Brought sheep into His fold.

_____
Write my name here.

(Answers are found on page 144.)

HERALD REPORTERS

Herald angels were a little like news reporters: they brought the great news of Christ's birth to all the world.

Read the following book after checking it out from your public library. Then do the follow-up activity by being a CHRISTMAS REPORTER.

GEORGIE'S CHRISTMAS CAROL
by Robert Bright
Doubleday & Co., Inc., 1975

Georgie's Christmas Carol is a sweet story fashioned after Dickens' classic tale, complete with a ghost, the amiable Georgie. Especially aimed at younger children, Robert Bright's delightful characters depict the ever-so-important feelings of Christmas: love, generosity, happiness, and joy. The wide-eyed innocence of young Tony and Sara helps not only their gloomy uncle, Mr. Gloams, but all of us to see the magical ability of Christmas to change people's lives.

Follow-up: ". . . freely ye have received, freely give." (Matthew 10:8)

Materials Needed: Strips of paper about 3'' x 18'', felt markers, writing paper and pencils, stapler

Activity: Sara and Tony found out what might make their uncle happy at Christmas simply by talking to him. Have the class members become Christmas reporters. Make each student a headband with the strips of paper. Write "Christmas Reporter" on each headband. Make interview pads by stapling several sheets of paper together. Challenge everyone to interview several adults about their past Christmases (joys and disappointments). Place special emphasis on talking to someone who is alone at Christmas (widows, single adults, etc.). Have the class decide on some standard interview questions ahead of time. When the class reports back, decide on one or two individuals for whom the class can do something special at Christmas that would help erase a past disappointment or bring back a previous joy.

BONUS ACTIVITY:

Write a news bulletin that might have been announced over the TV or radio about Christ's birth.

_____
_____
_____
_____
_____
_____
_____
_____

OBJECTIVE: To encourage children to recognize and praise others when they see them doing good deeds.

MATERIALS: Enlarged angel for one corner of the bulletin board. Pink paper for the background. Little clouds cut from construction paper.

PROCEDURE: Cover the board with the pink paper. Attach the enlarged angel and appropriate lettering near the top of the bulletin board. Conduct a class discussion about the ways we can show love by being good citizens and how important this is. Then explain that teachers do not always hear about each good deed that children do, as God does. Ask each class member to be a guardian angel for the other members of the class. Every time someone notices a classmate doing a kind deed, he or she records it on a small cloud and attaches it to the bulletin board. The students will be very proud when their classmates award them with written praises, and the bulletin board will be a constant reminder to all that good deeds do not go unnoticed.

SHEPHERDS

"And there were in the same country shepherds abiding in the field, keeping watch over their flock by night." Luke 2:8

At Christmas we celebrate the birth of the Good Shepherd. Christ often referred to Himself as a shepherd.

On the first Christmas night, shepherds played an important part in Christ's birth. They were among the very special few who were told the glorious news on the very night it happened!!

HEAR YOUR MASTER'S VOICE

Sheep are good listeners. They know their master's voice and can pick it out from many others.

Have one child be the master, the others the sheep. Let the master read the following passages of Scripture: Matt. 7:15, 9:36, 10:6, 12:12, 18:12; Mark 6:34, 14:27; Luke 2:8, 15:4; John 10:2.

The sheep should keep track of how many times the word *sheep* or *shepherd* is used. See which sheep is the best listener. Take turns being the master.

BLINDFOLD GAME— ANOTHER SHEEPISH ACTIVITY

Blindfold one child and put him in the center of the circle. Have the child in the circle call out the name of an animal. Select one child to act as master, who always calls out "sheep," no other animal. The child in the center must guess to whom the master's voice belongs. If he cannot guess after three tries, the master takes his place in the center and a new master is selected. If the child can guess his master's voice, he receives another turn in the center.

SELLING TO A SHEPHERD

Pretend you are a salesman living at the time of Jesus' birth in Bethlehem. There are many shepherds working in the surrounding hillsides.

Design a product that you think shepherds would need. It can be funny or serious, possible or impossible. Use your imagination.

Now draw a picture of your product here.

Design a billboard for your product here.

Write a magazine ad here.

Write a TV or radio commercial here.

SHEPHERD RECIPES

CANDY CANE COOKIES
(Shepherd Staffs)

1 egg
1 c. softened butter
¾ c. granulated sugar
1 tsp. peppermint extract
1 tsp. vanilla

2½ c. flour
1 tsp. baking powder
red sugar sprinkles
red food coloring

Beat together first 5 ingredients until fluffy.

Add flour and baking powder; beat well.

Divide dough into 2 equal portions. Stir ¾ tsp. red food coloring into one portion; mix well. For each cookie, shape 1 tsp. of each color dough into a 4-inch rope, rolling back and forth on waxed paper.

Place 1 red rope and 1 white rope side by side; press lightly and twist. Place 1 inch apart on ungreased cookie sheet. Curve one end of cookie down to form handle of candy cane. Brush with egg white; sprinkle with red sugar sprinkles.

Bake 8-10 minutes at 375⁰. Makes about 3 dozen 3-inch cookies.

SPICY SHEPHERD NUTS

1 cup granulated sugar
⅓ cup milk
½ teaspoon cinnamon
2½ cups walnuts

Bring first 3 ingredients to a boil until soft ball stage is reached (takes about 5 minutes). Add nuts; stir until coated. Turn out on foil; cool.

Shining Star Publications, Copyright © 1985, A division of Good Apple, Inc.

THE SHEPHERDS' STORY
Words and Music by Kathy Jones

"THE SHEPHERDS' STORY" ACTIVITIES

1. IT'S ALL OVER YOUR FACE

I wonder how the shepherds reacted to an angel from heaven appearing to them on that first Christmas Eve. It probably showed on their faces!

Have students practice showing different emotions with their faces. Have one person appear as an angel and say the words in Luke 2:10-12. The rest of the class reacts in different ways: surprise, fear, joy, perhaps even anger (maybe some shepherds were sleeping and didn't like being awakened). Have each emotion show on their faces! Take turns being the angel.

BONUS CHALLENGE: Make up other situations of your own. Write a short script for someone to say a few lines. Then let your face react to what's being said in different ways.

2. PRETTY AS A PICTURE

Have your class imagine what this glorious event must have looked like in a shepherd's field outside the little town of Bethlehem that first Christmas Eve. Now capture that beautiful picture on paper. Make it a big picture! On a long piece of butcher paper, have your class or family depict the shepherds' story. Include the hillsides, the town of Bethlehem in the distance, the sheep, the shepherds, the angelic hosts, the starry skies. Have each child submit a sketch and choose the best one, OR use a combination of sketches. Assign different groups to different portions of the mural.

3. YOUR OWN SHEPHERD STORY

Write your own shepherd story. The stories behind the stories sometimes are the best ones. Perhaps there was a little shepherd boy or girl on that hillside the night the angels came. Or perhaps one of the little lambs had a story he could have told about that first Christmas night. Write a story about what may have happened to your character on the day or days leading up to that first Christmas Eve, or maybe the morning after.

BONUS CHALLENGE: Make up a special song to go with your very own shepherd story.

THE SKY'S THE LIMIT

Shepherds who spent most of their time under the wide, blue heavens and starry skies must have used their imaginations a lot.

See if you can use YOUR imagination to get you in a Christmas-celebrating mood. THE SKY'S THE LIMIT.

CREATIVE ACTIVITY #1

Think of some kooky animals you might come up with by crossing a sheep with some other animal. Use SHEEP, LAMB, RAM, and EWE to do your crossing.

Examples: sheep + elephant = SHEEPEPHANT
          ram   + kangaroo = KANGARAM

The possibilities are endless. Write a story about shepherds and what they thought when some of your kooky, sheepish animals showed up in their flock!

_____ + _____ = _____

_____ + _____ = _____

_____ + _____ = _____

_____ + _____ = _____

_____ + _____ = _____

★★Keep on going on the back or on another sheet of paper.

CREATIVE ACTIVITY #2

Answer these questions; then substitute the word *I* for *shepherd*, and answer them again. How much do you remind yourself of a shepherd?

1. A shepherd reminds me of (what kind of animal)_____because _____
_____

2. A shepherd reminds me of (what kind of bird)_____because _____
_____

3. A shepherd reminds me of (what kind of fish)_____because _____
_____

4. A shepherd reminds me of (what kind of weather)_____because ____
_____

5. A shepherd reminds me of (what kind of fruit or vegetable) _____
because _____
_____

6. A shepherd reminds me of (what kind of plant or tree)_____because
_____

7. A shepherd reminds me of (what kind of flower)_____because _____
_____

SHEPHERD PUPPET FUN

Here are four different ways to have fun making paper puppets. When you make your puppets, put on a Bible puppet play. You can read Scripture or create lines for your puppet play.

Use a piece of construction paper and make yourself spoon puppets. Color and cut out a few puppet figures. Tape them to spoons. A table makes a dandy stage for spoon puppets.

Take a long envelope and place your hand inside it. Crease and fold the envelope in the center. Draw a face on the envelope. When you open and close your hand, you can make your puppet talk. Add a paper beard and a smaller version of the headdress idea on page 122.

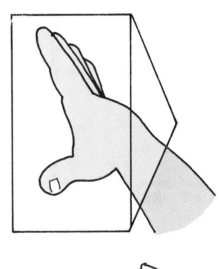

Want to have some high-stepping action? Try making a few of these walking, paper puppets. Just draw and cut out your puppets. Remember to allow enough room to cut two holes for your fingers. You can also have fun by letting your puppets move their arms.

holes for finger and thumb

holes for fingers

Use a piece of construction paper and cut out separate finger-puppet forms. Glue or tape the ends together. Draw your own puppet faces on the finger-puppet forms. You will have a handful of fun with this activity.

Now that you have been busy making puppets, you'll need some good ideas on making stages. Here are a few . . .

Have a production using a chair or a sofa as your stage.

Try a kitchen counter . . .

Make a cardboard box puppet stage. Cut out a stage opening on one side. The puppets are moved from the opening at the bottom. Draw in the stage curtains and background scenery.

a table or a bed headboard.

Have a puppet play using a window or a door . . . or a windowsill.

You can always string a rope up and drape a sheet on it.

CREATE A MAP

What if there were no stars or angels to guide the shepherds?

Design a shepherd's map leading out of the hills down into the town of Bethlehem, right to the stable where the shepherds found Mary, Joseph, and Baby Jesus.

Include rocks, trees, buildings, streets, and anything else the shepherds might use as guideposts to help them find their way back to their flocks.

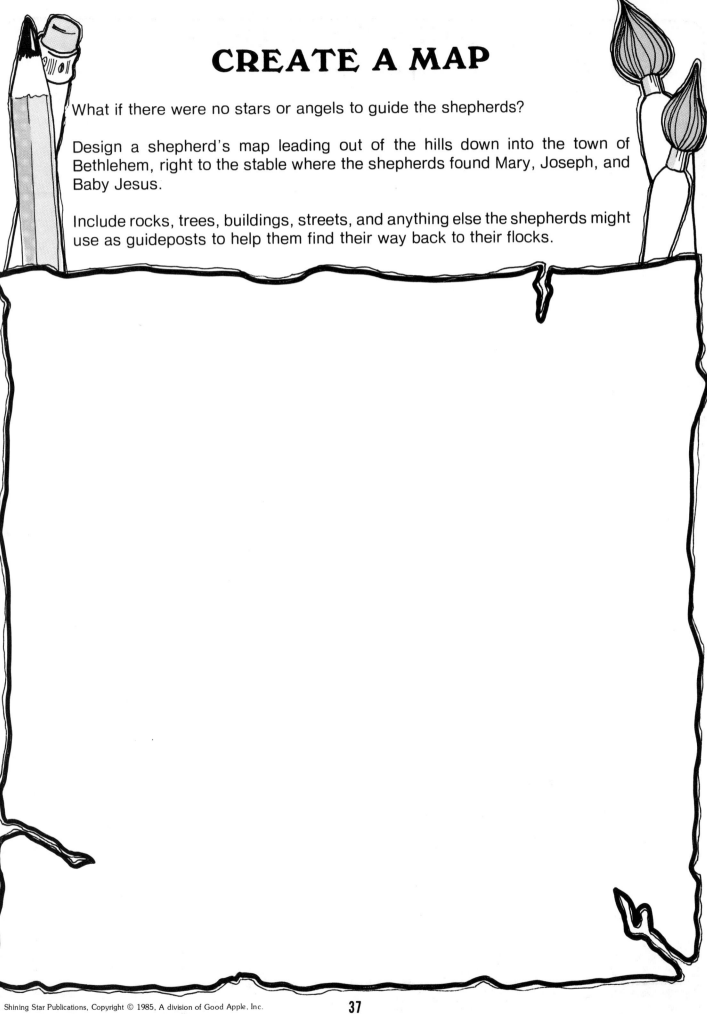

DESIGN YOUR OWN

The shepherds received the best kind of Christmas greeting card—one straight from heaven!

Design your own greeting card. Pretend you're an angel. Re-read Luke 2:9-17. Now what will YOUR greeting from heaven say?

FRONT OF CARD   **INSIDE MESSAGE**

Now that you've designed it, make it!

★ STARS

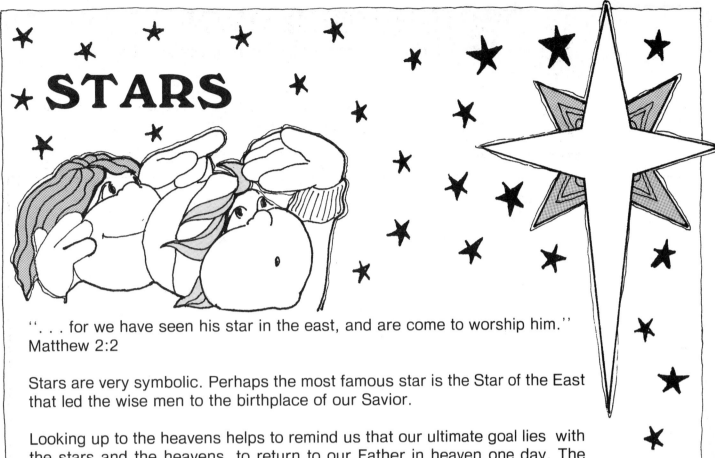

"... for we have seen his star in the east, and are come to worship him."
Matthew 2:2

Stars are very symbolic. Perhaps the most famous star is the Star of the East that led the wise men to the birthplace of our Savior.

Looking up to the heavens helps to remind us that our ultimate goal lies with the stars and the heavens, to return to our Father in heaven one day. The beautiful starry skies that God has created for us keeps our minds on lofty goals. May the star of Christmas keep our sights high forever!

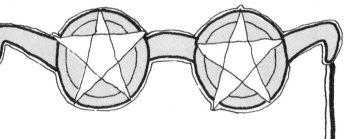

STARRY-EYED

Stars are used in so many ways and in so many places. We call someone who has reached the top of his field a STAR; someone who has done even better is called a SUPER STAR.

Make a list of STARS and SUPER STARS whom you know or admire. They can be from the area of sports, the arts, the Bible, living or dead.

Next to each name on your list, write why you think that person became a star.

REACH FOR A STAR

Words and Music by
Kathy Jones

"REACH FOR A STAR" ACTIVITIES

Christmas stars can remind us how important it is to always be REACHING FOR A STAR. Christmas also reminds us that a NEW YEAR is just around the corner, a good time for making goals that will help us to REACH FOR A STAR.

THE SKY'S THE LIMIT

Have a goal-setting session in your class or family before Christmas. Place each goal (individual or group) on a star-shaped cutout. You can color code your stars as to type of goals.

Example:
        personal goals - blue stars
        spiritual goals - silver stars
        physical goals - green stars
        intellectual goals - red stars

Now display your stars on a bulletin board or hang them by strings from the ceiling. If you need a reminder about what goals you set for yourself, just "reach for a star." Decorating them with glitter will add to your Christmas decor.

If you have some goals you want to keep private, that's okay. Put your star away in a secret place or paste two stars together before putting on display.

HALFWAY HARRY   HALFWAY HANNAH

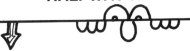

STARTING DATE
_____

HALFWAY

GOAL

START THE YEAR WITH A CLEAN SLATE

MATERIALS:

black construction paper
white construction paper
white chalk
chalk fixative
pen

Give each student a sheet of black construction paper and a piece of white chalk. Have each student write one New Year's resolution on his "slate" and draw a frame around it. Spray each paper with a chalk fixative to curtail smearing.

Encourage the children to trust God to help them keep their resolutions. Give each child a piece of white paper cut to resemble a piece of chalk. On the "chalk," have him copy a Scripture verse declaring God's ever present help.

HALFWAY HARRY (OR HANNAH)

Half the fun of reaching your goals is in the trying. Like the song says, ". . . you'll find the feeling sublime." Make a chart like the one shown in the illustration. Figure out some halfway goals to measure your progress.

Remember, it's okay if you don't reach a goal as soon as you'd hoped, and it's okay if you have to change your goal a little. Arriving halfway there is a lot better than never starting at all!

Reaching a goal is one of the best Christmas gifts you can give yourself!

VERSES MAY INCLUDE:

Ps. 40:17	Ps. 46:1
II Chron. 25:8	Ps. 33:20
Ps. 121:2	Ps. 37:40
I Sam. 7:12	Ps. 27:1
Rom. 8:26	Heb. 13:6
Ps. 124:8	

Display each "slate and chalk" on a bulletin board.

YOU CAN DO ANYTHING! MORE ACTIVITIES

Only three specific goals are mentioned in the song: '' . . . play a bassoon, write a new tune, fly to the moon . . . .'' Write some more verses to the song patterned after verse two. Here are some ideas to get you going:

> play a new part
> heal a sick heart
> be first to start
> or paint some great art
>
> pitch a baseball
> build a great hall (wall)
> invent a new doll
>
> run in the race
> make lovely lace
> sketch a new face

Let your imagination soar!

You can do anything!

FOR MUSIC LOVERS NATURALLY

Notice in the eighth measure of the song there is an A natural. Normally, this note is played as A-flat, but here it is a natural A. Be careful when you sing it.

If you play an instrument, read music a little, or just like to sing, go on a ''natural hunt.'' Find some other songs in hymn books, sheet music or song books that you may have at home or church. Look for the natural sign and practice singing those notes very carefully. Do they sound different?

VOCATION NOTATION

''You can . . . be anything . . . .'' Conduct a survey of your class members, family members, friends and relatives. Some young people already have a pretty good idea of what they want to be in life. Find out what vocations are most popular, most interesting, most unusual. Share your findings with your class or family.

STAR TRACK

Make a whole series of numbered stars and cover them with Con-Tact paper to protect them. There should be several stars of each numeral. Then in certain patterns and paths around the room or from room to room make a ''star track.'' For instance, make a path of stars with the number 6 to the sandbox or a track of number 3 stars to the housekeeping area. This activity could be made into a kind of treasure hunt with a surprise at the end. At the starting point, give each child a star with ''his'' numeral on it to follow. The treasure at the end might be a chance to make a spaceship from egg cartons, margarine tubs, and glue or to create the moon surface from sand and water. This game may be done in pairs, groups, or solo. The main idea is to get the children to look for and recognize ''their'' numbers and to follow them.

STAR LIGHT, STAR BRIGHT

Give each child a dark piece of paper with a quarter or half-moon pasted on it. Write a numeral on the moon. Have the child take pre-pasted gummy stars (available in almost any school supply or variety store) and put the appropriate number of stars in the sky. The larger stars are easier for young children to handle.

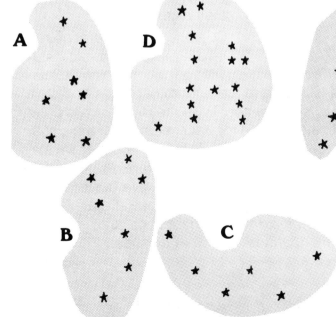

A   D

E

B   C   F

CONNECT

Connect the stars to make each constellation of stars. Find each one in the sky. Write its name.

(Answers are found on page 144.)

A STAR-STUDDED STORY

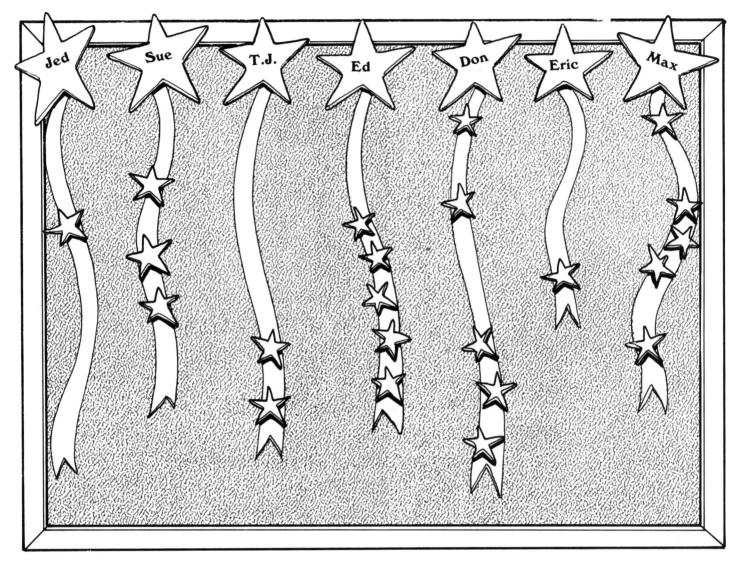

OBJECTIVE: To encourage students to memorize Bible verses in Luke 2, the Christmas story.

MATERIALS: Paper stars, glue, glitter, memory verses on small slips of paper.

PROCEDURE: Cover bulletin board with dark blue paper. Cut enough stars so each member of the class has one big star and 20 small ones. Write each student's name on a big star and attach the stars along the top of the bulletin board. Attach a piece of Christmas ribbon to the bottom of each name star. Decorate the little stars with lots of silver glitter. Type the Bible verses Luke 2:1-20 on a sheet of paper. Duplicate enough for each member of the class. Then cut the verses apart so you can give each child one or two of them at a time. Allow each child to decide how many verses she plans to memorize during the week. When the student can recite a verse, give her a glitter-covered star to hang on the ribbon dangling from her special star. These verses are short and when the child knows this chapter of Luke, she will always have the true meaning of Christmas etched in her heart.

STAR MOSAIC

Try your hand at creating two of the earliest church art forms still seen in many of our modern churches.

Many of the interiors of sixteenth century Christian churches were decorated with mosaics. When Byzantine Emperor Justinian captured Italy, the city of Ravenna became a center of Byzantine culture. In Ravenna there are many examples of ornate pictures made from small tiles of colored glass or stone that were set in cement. As the light reflected from this shiny work of art, a lighted tapestry effect resulted.

You can make your own mosaic with the following materials:

1. a bag of uncooked rice
2. various glass or plastic bowls
3. food coloring (red, blue, yellow, green)
4. cardboard paper
5. glue, pencil and markers (red, blue, yellow, green)

Put the rice in four separate bowls. Add a few drops of the coloring to each of the bowls and stir. Allow a few minutes for the rice to dry. The rice will then be used as mosaic pieces.

Draw your star design on the piece of cardboard. Divide your star into sections and color each section. Apply glue to those areas to which you want the rice to stick. This is best done by placing the glue on all the blue areas and sprinkling the blue rice on this area. Then apply glue to the red area and sprinkle the red rice on these sections. Continue until the picture is completed.

MOBILE DIRECTIONS:

1. Remove the label and the plastic base from a plastic soda bottle. (Some soda bottles do not have removable bases.)
2. Cut the top of the bottle off about four inches from the top. Punch holes along the edge.
3. Cut various shaped pieces from the bottom half of the bottle. Stars, triangles, squares and fish are easy shapes to cut.
4. Color these pieces. Punch a hole at both ends of the shapes.
5. Attach the shapes with string to the soda top as shown.
6. Attach a string to the top and hang your star mobile in an attractive place.

STARS BULLETIN BOARD

Have the children look at the starry sky before doing this project.

Put black craft paper on one wall or bulletin board area of the classroom. Discuss the fact that most stars look white, red or blue and that some look larger and brighter than others.

Have the children cut lots of red, white and blue stars from paper and glue them on the black background. You may want to include illustrations of major constellations.

A discussion about galaxies and the Milky Way might follow. The children do not have to memorize the names of the stars, but after this unit they may become more aware of the wonders of the night sky.

SUGAR COOKIE STARS

1 ⅓ cups of butter
1 ½ cups granulated sugar
1 teaspoon vanilla
2 eggs
3 tablespoons milk
1 tablespoon baking powder
4 cups of flour
½ teaspoon salt

Thoroughly cream butter, sugar and vanilla.
Add eggs and beat till light and fluffy.
Stir in the milk.
Sift together the dry ingredients.
Blend into creamed mixture.
Divide the dough in quarters and chill 1 hour.

On a slightly floured surface, roll dough to a 1/8-inch thickness. Use a star-shaped cookie cutter to cut the cookes. Each child can cut out his own cookie.

Bake on a greased cookie sheet at 375 degrees for 6-8 minutes. Sprinkle warm cookies with red or green sugar sparkles.

DECORATING TIPS: If using red, green, or multi-colored sprinkles, SPRINKLE BEFORE BAKING.

Red or green-colored frosting can be easily made by using 1 cup of confectioners' sugar and adding milk, 1 tsp. at a time, until desired consistency is reached. Then add food coloring.

WINDOW PANE cookies can be made by cutting a hole in the cut cookies before baking and placing them on aluminum foil on the cookie sheet. Place a few pieces of crushed life savers in the hole. Bake; cool; peel off foil.

SUPER STAR TARTS

1 pkg. refrigerated roll cookie dough (sugar or peanut butter)
1 box miniature peanut butter cups.

Slice the cookie dough roll into 9 slices. Cut each slice into four pieces. Roll each piece into a ball and drop into greased miniature muffin tin, one ball for each section. Bake at 375 degrees for 10 minutes. While cookies are baking, remove paper from peanut butter cups. As soon as the cookies come out of the oven, press a peanut butter cup into the center of each cookie. Let cool. This make 36 cookies that look like tarts.

SUPER STAR FUDGE

4½ cups sugar
1 13-ounce can evaporated milk
18 oz. of semi-sweet chocolate chips
1 jar marshmallow cream
1 cup butter or margarine

2 tsp. vanilla
1½ cups chopped nuts

Bring sugar and milk to a rolling boil in a large pan; boil for 5-8 minutes, stirring constantly.

In a large bowl, place the rest of the ingredients EXCEPT the nuts and vanilla. Pour hot mixture into bowl; beat with electric mixture until smooth; stir in nuts and vanilla.

Spread into 9 x 13 greased pan; chill at least 3 hours. Cut and serve.

SOME STARS TO FOLD

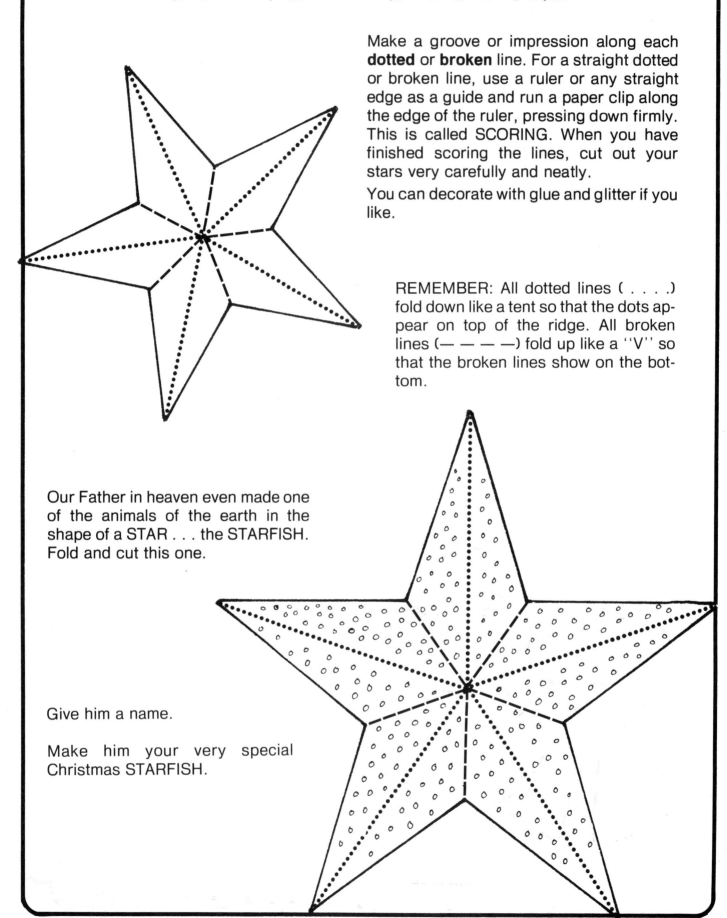

Make a groove or impression along each **dotted** or **broken** line. For a straight dotted or broken line, use a ruler or any straight edge as a guide and run a paper clip along the edge of the ruler, pressing down firmly. This is called SCORING. When you have finished scoring the lines, cut out your stars very carefully and neatly.

You can decorate with glue and glitter if you like.

REMEMBER: All dotted lines (. . . .) fold down like a tent so that the dots appear on top of the ridge. All broken lines (— — — —) fold up like a "V" so that the broken lines show on the bottom.

Our Father in heaven even made one of the animals of the earth in the shape of a STAR . . . the STARFISH. Fold and cut this one.

Give him a name.

Make him your very special Christmas STARFISH.

STAR STAINED-GLASS WINDOW

Cut stars from colored pieces of cellophane. Tape them to the windows so that the sun will shine through the cellophane and make star patterns in the classroom.

"Twinkle, twinkle, little star,

How I wonder what you are."

HOW TO DRAW A FIVE-POINTED STAR

1. Draw 2 sides of a triangle.
2. Draw a line from the lower right corner that crosses the center of the other line.
3. Draw a line straight across that crosses the other side halfway.
4. Close the star by connecting the last line drawn with the corner of the first line.

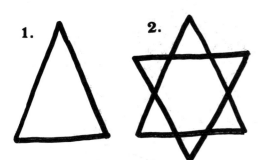

HOW TO DRAW A SIX-POINTED STAR

1. Draw a triangle.
2. Draw another triangle upside down and centered over the first one.

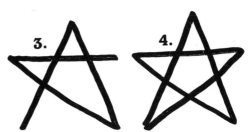

STAR POETRY

Star light, star bright,
First star I've seen tonight.
Wish I may, wish I might
Make a wish come true tonight.

Draw a picture of your wish.

COOKING CRYSTAL ORNAMENTS

MATERIALS NEEDED:

1. Several packages of "cooking crystals." These are bits of colored plastic that melt when placed in an oven. They can be bought in art and hobby shops.
2. Dough-salt mixture made from the following recipe:
   ⅔ cup of salt
   ⅔ cup of flour
   ½ cup of water
   Mix these ingredients thoroughly.
3. Cookie cutters and knives
4. Aluminum foil
5. Cookie sheet
6. Paper clips

DIRECTIONS:

Cover the cookie sheet with the foil. Give each child a portion of the dough mixture to design an ornament using the cookie cutter. Have him roll the dough flat and cut out the shapes.

Then, using a butter knife, cut away the inside portion of the shapes. Leave about ½ inch around the edges.

Place these figures on the cookie sheet and bake at 350 degrees for fifteen minutes. Remove from the oven and add the crystals to the inside of each shape. Place a paper clip in the top of each ornament. The clips will be used to hang the ornaments. When baked, these crystals will melt and create shiny see-through ornaments.

Read the directions on the crystals' package to see how long to bake the ornaments. Let them cool; then carefully remove them from the sheet.

This recipe can be used for any shape of ornament.

Other shapes may be used for your Christmas couplets.

CHRISTMAS COUPLETS

Christmas green, Christmas red,
By a star wise men were led.

A couplet is a two-line poem that rhymes. To write a Christmas couplet, you must write the word *Christmas* two times in the first line. Each time, follow the word *Christmas* with a color. The second line must rhyme with the first. Write your couplet within a Christmas design or shape, or use the verse as part of an original Christmas card.

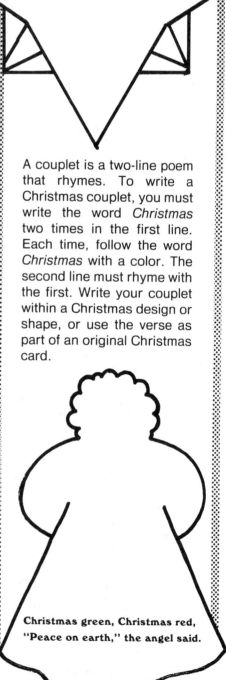

Christmas green, Christmas red,
"Peace on earth," the angel said.

HOW MANY STARS?

Even though there were many stars in the heavens on the way to Bethlehem, the wise men were still able to pick out the ONE STAR that would lead them to their King!

How many stars can you pick out of this puzzle?

(The answer is found on page 144.)

STAR MAN

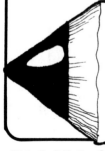

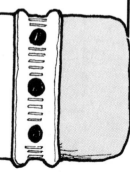

On this page, draw a picture of a man (or woman) completely made of stars—star eyes, star ears, star nose, star hair, star feet! When you are finished, count all the stars on your STAR MAN . . . . See who has the starriest man!

AT THE INN

IMAGINE THAT NIGHT

"And she brought forth her first born son, and wrapped him in swaddling clothes, and laid him in a manger; because there was no room for them in the inn."

OBJECTIVE: To encourage children to imagine and experience the fact that Jesus, our Lord, was born in a stable.

MATERIALS: Large pattern of the Mary and Babe found on this page. (Make a transparency and use an overhead projector to make a pattern the size you need.) Blue paper for background and the appropriate Bible verse. Large drawing paper and paints or crayons.

PROCEDURE: Cover bulletin board with light blue paper. Attach the large pattern of Mary and Baby Jesus. Print the Bible verse, Luke 2:7, at the top of the board. Then read the Christmas story to your children. Ask them to visualize the night Jesus was born. List the animals that may have been present in the stable. Talk about the other objects that would have been part of the setting. After you complete the story, ask the children to create a large animal or other object that may have been in the stable on the first Christmas Eve. Encourage all new ideas. Attach the animals and other objects to the board to complete the picture.

GIFT OF GIFTS

Verse three of the song "Within a Lowly Stable," p. 56, mentions the kings who would worship Baby Jesus. Read Matthew 2:1-15. They brought treasures of great value to give to Him. Play a recording of the song "Little Drummer Boy," or find a copy of the music and teach it to the class. Discuss the important elements in both the gifts of the kings and that of the drummer boy. Have each class member write about or draw what he might have given Baby Jesus as a token of love had he lived at the time of Jesus' birth. Then have each student write about or draw what he might give today to show his love for Jesus now. Have this project serve as a personal challenge for this Christmas season.

NATIVITY SCENE
(Matthew 1 and Luke 2)

FOLD

Making this nativity scene isn't difficult, and the results will surprise everyone! First, make sure you have a tissue box, aluminum foil, pipe cleaner, star-shaped pattern (see page 49), gold or white crayons, scissors and tape.

Cut away the top panel of the tissue box. Use the foil to cover the inside of the box. Color and cut out Jesus' family. Tape them near the back of the box. Cut out the sheep. Tape near the front of the box. Tape the star to the pipe cleaner. Tape the pipe cleaner to the back of the box at the center. Cut out and tape on other figures, such as the angel, shepherd, and cattle. If you wish, draw, cut out and tape on wise men, donkeys, etc.

FOLD

FOLD BACK HERE

FOLD

FOLD

IN A MANGER
Words and Music
by
Kathy J. Jones

55

WITHIN A LOWLY STABLE
Words and Music by Kathy Jones

Verse 3.　　Within a lowly stable was heard a distant bell.
　　　　　　Within a lowly stable the story shepherds tell.
　　　　　　Kings would bow before Him now; He would be called Emmanuel.
　　　　　　Within a lowly stable was heard a distant bell.

"WITHIN A LOWLY STABLE" ACTIVITIES

Practice this song as a family for several weeks. Present it in church or to your own extended family on Christmas Eve. The men in the family could sing the parts about shepherds and kings with the girls singing the phrases about angels and Mary. All could sing the repetitive phrase "within a lowly stable." Costumes would add a special touch.

STAR OF BETHLEHEM

In verse 2 of the song, stars are mentioned. Find the Scripture in Matthew which tells of the special star which led the wise men to the infant King. Have the class make star decorations for their trees at home and one special star representing the Star of the East. Have available several patterns, glue, glitter, sequins, and scissors.

STABLE VISIT

Hold a class discussion on why the children think Jesus was born in a stable instead of in a palace. List the characteristics of a stable. Then, if possible, arrange for the class to visit an actual stable. How would it have felt to bear a child in such a place? Conduct a creative writing activity where the children write modern day stories about a child born in a stable. Share the stories.

FLANNEL BOARD STORY: THE FIRST CHRISTMAS

Here is a simple flannel board story of the first Christmas that can be easily memorized and given even by young children with the help of the flannel board cutouts.

*Each time the word *cutout* is used, place the appropriate cutout on the flannel board.

Once upon a time, long ago in the city of Nazareth, lived a man named Joseph (cutout).

An angel of the Lord (cutout) appeared to Joseph and told him to take Mary (cutout) as his wife. She was going to have a Baby, who would be the Son of God.

Just before Mary had the Baby, Joseph took her to Bethlehem on a donkey (cutout). It was a long journey and hard for Mary.

When they got to Bethlehem, they could find no place to stay for the night. There was no room in the inn, but the innkeeper said they could sleep in the stable out back (cutout).

That night, that very special night, Baby Jesus was born, Savior to all the world. Mary wrapped Him in swaddling clothes and laid Him in a manger (cutout).

An angel of the Lord appeared to some shepherds who were just outside of Bethlehem watching their flocks of sheep (cutout). The angel told them of the wonderful birth. Many angels were singing (cutout). Many people came to see the newborn baby, Savior to all the world. In the stable, oxen, a donkey, lambs and doves were there to welcome Him (cutout). Shepherds may have come (cutout), village folk and wise men, too (cutout). All of them wanted to come and worship the newborn King. King Herod (cutout) said he wanted to worship the new King, too, but the wise men knew better. The first Christmas was very special. We can make all our Christmases just as special if we always remember what took place on the first Christmas.

VILLAGE FOLK

MARY ON DONKEY

FLANNEL BOARD CUTOUTS

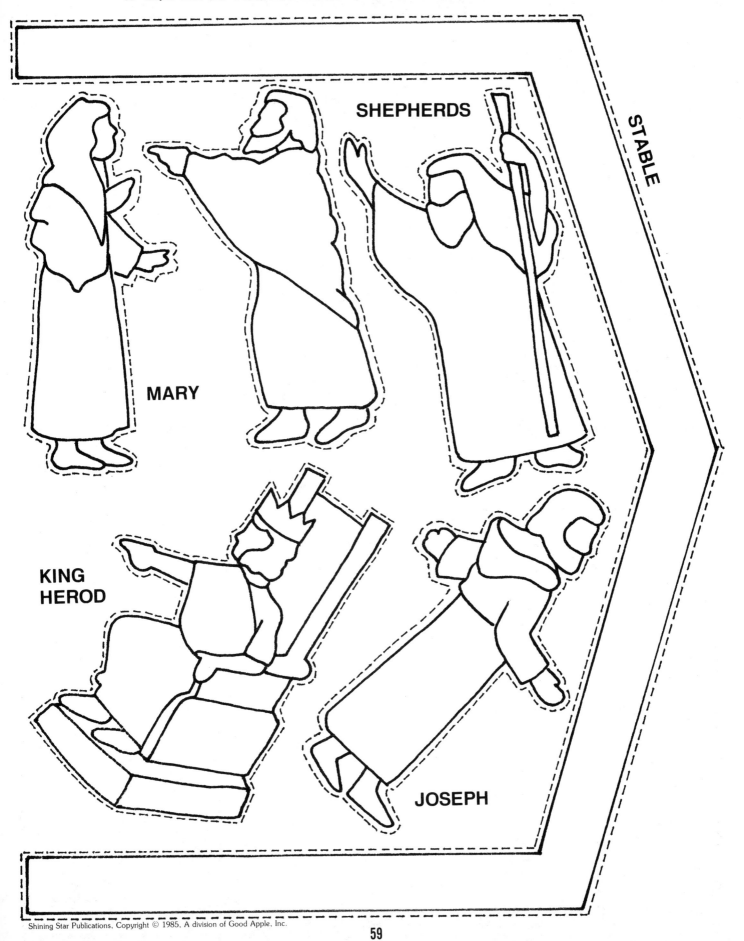

STABLE

SHEPHERDS

MARY

KING
HEROD

JOSEPH

FLANNEL BOARD CUTOUTS

ANGELIC HOST

DOVES

GOLD

GIFTS OF WISE MEN

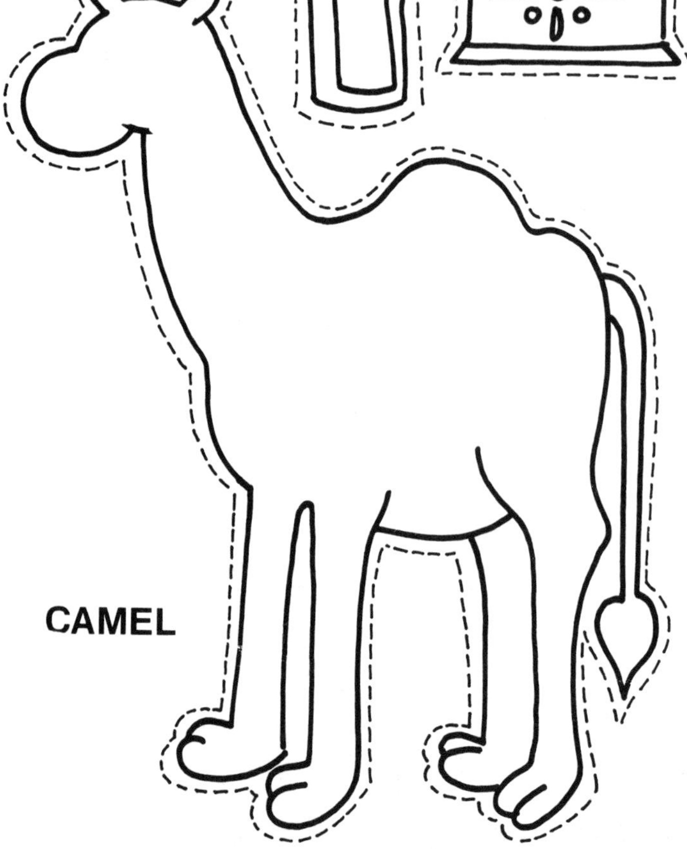

HERALD ANGEL

CAMEL

FLANNEL BOARD CUTOUTS

THREE WISE MEN

DONKEY

BABY JESUS IN MANGER

CATTLE/OXEN

LAMB/SHEEP

STAR

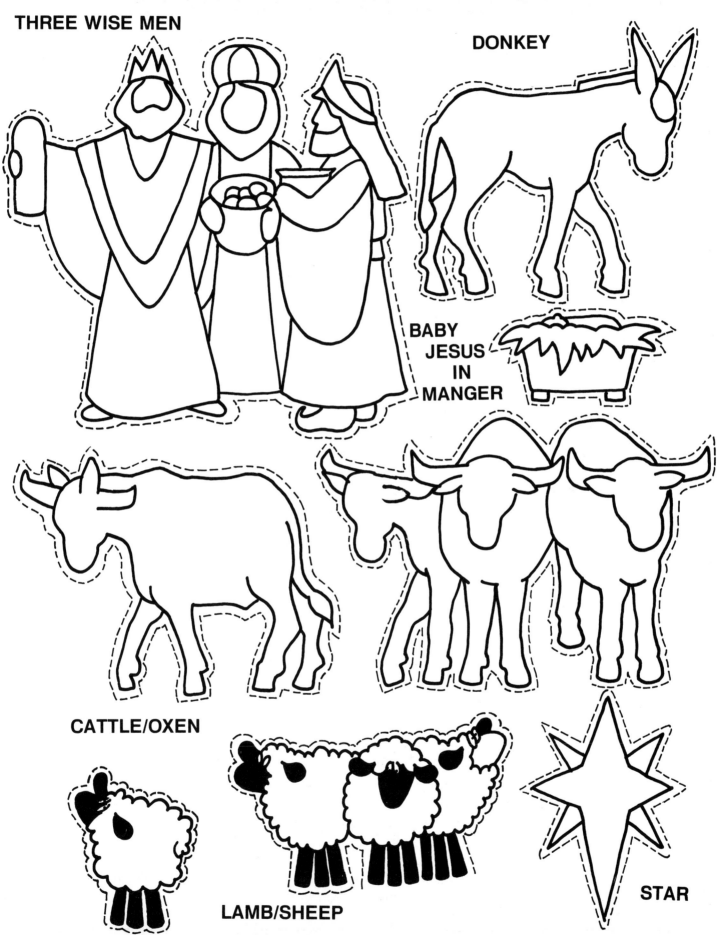

NATIVITY CRAFTS

Joseph may have needed light in the stable on that first Christmas night when Jesus was born.

Perhaps he used a lantern. Perhaps he used a candle.

Follow the directions below and make your own Christmas candle to remember the small light Joseph used in the stable on that night so long ago.

CHRISTMAS CANDLE

Materials:
1. cardboard milk cartons, half-pint size
2. birthday cake candles
3. paraffin blocks
4. broken pieces of red or green crayons
5. saucepan or large tin can
6. wooden stick for stirring

Directions:
Cut milk cartons down to a height of 3 inches.
In a saucepan or large tin can (bent to form a pouring lip),
slowly melt 2 blocks of paraffin. Add broken pieces of red or green wax crayons. Stir with a stick until they are melted and blended together. Pour this mixture into the carton molds until half full. When wax begins to set, put a birthday candle into the center of each wax mold. Allow wax to become rather firm. Then pour more melted wax to the height of the birthday candle wick. Set the molds in a cool place to harden. After 2 days remove the cardboard cartons. Decorate candles with whipped soap flakes or unusual sequins. Pin the sequins to the candle with straight pins. These candles make pretty gifts for mothers.

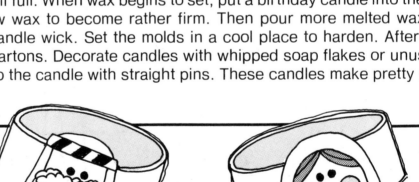

NATIVITY NAPKIN RINGS

Materials: old toilet paper rolls, paper scraps, markers
Directions: Cut the toilet paper rolls into one-inch strips. You will need one for each person who will be having Christmas dinner with you.
Use a half-dollar to make circles for faces.
Decorate the faces to look like Mary, Joseph, and Baby Jesus. Depending on how many there are in your family, add angels, shepherds, wise men, etc.
Glue each face to a paper ring. When you set the table for Christmas, put a napkin in each ring.

**C IS FOR CHRISTMAS. C IS FOR COLOR.
COLOR THIS PICTURE OF THE FIRST CHRISTMAS.**

CREATIVE WRITING SKILLS

PICK ONE OF THE CHRISTMAS STORY IDEAS BELOW AND WRITE A SHORT STORY OF YOUR OWN. CIRCLE YOUR CHOICE.

1 What might have happened if . . .
   a. you had been in the town of Bethlehem on that first Christmas Eve?
   b. you had been one of the shepherds who saw the star and heard the angels sing?
   c. you had been one of the wise men who followed the star to Bethlehem?
   d. you had been one of the animals in the stable behind the inn?

2 Write a story about an alien coming to Earth during our Christmas season. Perhaps your story could begin with two men from Mars (or some other planet) who have been commissioned to find out why Earthlings celebrate Christmas.

3 Write a story or poem that begins "If I were . . .
   a. the Star of Bethlehem . . . ."
   b. the innkeeper on Christmas Eve . . . ."
   c. an angel on Christmas Eve . . . ."
   d. Mary or Joseph . . . ."
Write what you would see, hear and feel on that special night.

_____
_____
_____
_____
_____
_____
_____
_____
_____
_____
_____
_____
_____
_____
_____
_____
_____
_____

WISE MEN, BRAVE MEN

"... behold, there came wise men from the east to Jerusalem, Saying, Where is he that is born King of the Jews...." Matthew 2:1-2

We are not at all sure how many wise men searched for Baby Jesus. Our traditions tell us three because of the three gifts presented to Him. Ever since that first Christmas and the example set by these brave men, we have all continued to give one another gifts at Christmastime.

JOURNEY OF THE KINGS

Learn the words to the familiar Christmas carol "We Three Kings."

Notice the words *field and fountain, moor and mountain.*

Look up any words you are unsure of in the dictionary. Get a picture in your mind of what this long, long journey looked like.

On a large piece of manila paper, do a watercolor background, a "wash" that would make you think of fields, fountains, moors, or mountains.

Use the cutouts on page 61 to make some paper doll figures of your three kings (wise men). "Dress" them with scraps of material, trim, sequins that you might have around the house. Glue them to your "wash" background. Draw camels if you like.

THE CAMEL WALK

See if you can walk like a camel. Play the music to "We Three Kings" while you are trying your camel walk.

Find pictures of camels and all the information you can about these kingly beasts. Make a short one-page report.

WISE MEN, BRAVE MEN
(A Round for Christmas)
Words and Music by Kathy J. Jones

3. Wise men, brave men,
Forewarned in a dream;
Kings and rulers
Are not what they seem.

Do not tell King Herod
That you found your King.
Journey home and spread
The glad news that you bring.

"WISE MEN, BRAVE MEN" ACTIVITIES

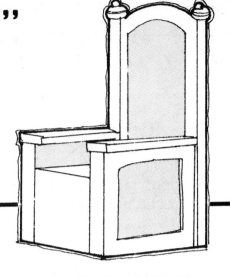

KING HEROD'S COURT

King Herod did some wicked things. Find out what he did that the wise men were forewarned about in their dream by reading the entire second chapter of Matthew.

Draw a picture of what you think King Herod's court may have looked like with King Herod on his throne.

LONG, LONG JOURNEY

We aren't sure just exactly how far the wise men had to travel. But we know they must have had to travel a very long distance from somewhere. With an old shoe box or another box of similar size turned on its side, make a diorama of some part of the wise men's journey. First, paint or draw the background on paper and then glue it into place in the box. Remember to cover the bottom, top and sides of the inside of the box as it sits on its side. Decide whether your scene will be of a town they passed through, King Herod's court, the desert, etc., and whether it was day or night. You could use dark blue or black tissue paper for a night sky, glitter for stars, construction paper for sun or moon. Bits of real grass or leaves could be used for landscaping. Then, in your diorama, place pipe cleaner figures of your wise men covered with scraps of cloth to represent their clothing. Pipe cleaner camels or horses could also be used to complete your diorama.

GIFTS FOR A KING

The song tells of two of the gifts that the wise men brought when they found the infant King. Do you know what the third gift was? Matthew 2:11 tells you the answer.

With some empty boxes of various shapes, plan to make a gift that you would like to offer to Baby Jesus this Christmas. Decorate your box with foil, glitter, discarded costume jewelry, sequins, and anything that you feel might make it look as if something of value is inside. Then decide what treasure you have that you will give to the infant King. Perhaps it will be a small heart to show that you will try harder to show love to someone this next year or a picture of a smiling face to show Him you intend to spread more happiness. It doesn't have to be an elaborate gift. Make it something to show Baby Jesus you love Him and care about other people, too!

... MORE ACTIVITIES

RECORD YOUR ROUND

If your group is not large enough to sing the song effectively as a round, get a cassette tape recorder and record the song, singing all three verses once through. Now play it back and sing against the tape recorder, coming in at the third measure marked with a no. 2. Sing softly enough against the tape recorder so that you can hear your harmonizing. Happy rounding!

WISE MEN, BRAVE MEN

These men were very brave to have journeyed such a long distance in search of the infant King. What adventures they must have had! In your class or family, start a group story about an adventure they might have had during their travels. Use a bell or timer to signal the next person's turn to take up the story where the last person left off. Have the last person in the group finish the story. Try it again. King Herod may have provided these wise men with some exciting adventures when he discovered their deception!

PERIL IN PANTOMIME

While the song is being sung, have several children pantomime the actions of these ''wise men, brave men.'' Start with ''Following the Star''; then pantomime the wise men deciding if they should ask King Herod, talking to King Herod, finding the Christ Child, receiving their dream of warning. Costumes and props could add to the fun!

WE THREE KINGS
(A PANTOMIME)

Cast of Characters

King 1   Joseph
King 2   Mary
King 3   Christ Child

Setting: on road just outside city of Bethlehem; three wise men enter from side leading donkeys; all pause to rest.

KING #1:   (Looks up and points to star.)

KING #2:   (Gestures to others to follow.)

ALL 3:   (Walk as if to travel some distance, occasionally gesturing upward towards star in the East; at last arrive in Bethlehem; find Joseph standing in doorway.)

JOSEPH: (Looks up as kings approach; nods and smiles.)

KING #3:   (Points up to star shining down on rooftop, then to Joseph; turns to companions as if to confer with them.)

KING #2:   (Walks up to Joseph; gestures toward doorway as if to ask a question.)

KING #1:   (Approaches Joseph and points to star; Joseph's eyes turn upward.)

KING #3:   (Ties up animals then joins the rest.)

JOSEPH: (Gestures toward doorway as if to invite the three travelers inside.)

MARY: (Seated with Baby Jesus cradled in her arms; looks up as wise men enter.)

ALL 3:   (Bow low before the Christ Child and present their gifts, one at a time.)

JOSEPH: (Walks behind Mary; puts hands on her shoulders and looks down at Baby.)

Shining Star Publications, Copyright © 1985. A division of Good Apple, Inc.

QUEST OF THE WISE MEN

On a night so long ago
    Wise men traveled from afar.
Did they wonder, did they know
    Where would lead that shining star?

Over mountains, over plains,
    On and on their camels walked.
Thirst and hunger, aches and pains—
    Every night they talked and talked . . .

Of the wondrous star above,
    Of the dream that each had dreamed:
Prophecy of God's great love.
    Was it closer than it seemed?

Asking king to help their quest,
    Would it bring them closer still?
Wise men wondered, ''Was it best?''
    On they went through dark and chill.

Finally the star stood still;
    On a humble house it shone.
Father Joseph stopped them 'til
    Each had made his purpose known.

''Speak in whispers, bend your knee.''
    Before the blessed Babe they bow.
Gifts of finest quality
    Brought to Him to honor now—

Prince of Peace, King of Kings,
    Savior, Lord o'er all the earth.
Hear the herald angels sing,
    ''Blessed day of Jesus' birth!''

"QUEST OF THE WISE MEN" ACTIVITIES

This poem can be read aloud to the children, OR the children can read it themselves as a group if used as a choral reading. One way to use it would be to let the boys read one stanza aloud and the girls read the next. Another grouping might include seven groups of an equal number of children or a separate group to represent the lines the wise men themselves most likely would say.

Have the children illustrate the story as a class by creating a ROLLER BOX STORY.

MATERIALS:

A large pasteboard box or carton; two sticks or broom handles about 6'' longer than the box is wide (or use empty cardboard tubes); a roll of wrapping paper or freezer wrap (Freezer wrap is best for removing paper later.)

DIRECTIONS:

Be sure the box is large enough so that an opening may be cut in one side big enough to display children's drawings. Cut an opening in the bottom of the box for your display. Measure 4 inches up from the bottom of the box and 4 inches down from the top on each side. Cut round holes at these points and push the broom sticks or tubes through them.

Attach a long roll of wrapping paper or freezer wrap to the rollers. Tape the pictures the children draw on this background paper and write the captions underneath the pictures. Space the pictures so that you see one at a time as you turn the roller.

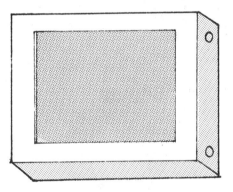 

Children can make their own roller boxes from small empty gelatin boxes. Cut a window in one side of the box and lay the box, window side up, on a 10-inch square of aluminum foil. Fold the foil around the box and tuck into the window. Slide a used pencil through the box (from top to bottom) at each end. Children may then use long strips of paper (about 2 inches wide) to make their own stories or to draw scenes from the Bible. Attach the strips to the pencils with cellophane tape.

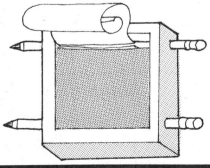 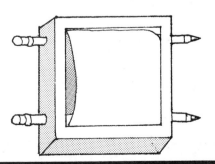

WHAT MAKES WISE MEN WISE?

There are two kinds of people in the Christmas story as recorded by Matthew in chapter two: the GIVERS (like the wise men) and the TAKERS (like King Herod).

Cut out the faces below and glue each face on separate tongue depressors.

Cut out the word strips below and paste them under the right faces. What makes WISE MEN WISE? What makes WICKED MEN WICKED?

Write a modern day Christmas story about a GIVER and a TAKER: someone who was wise enough to know what Christmas is all about and someone who had yet to learn that important lesson. If you can, put yourself in your story.

LOVE	TRUTH	HONESTY
SPIRITUALITY	LIES	GOOD WILL
GIVING HEART	COURAGE	MURDER
HATRED	PRIDE	TRUST
DECEIT	DISTRUST	PRAYER

CREATIVE WRITING SKILLS

WE THREE KINGS

The Bible tells us very little about the wise men who searched for the newborn Messiah. We are not even sure if there were three or some other number of people.

For the moment, let's say there were three men. Sing the familiar Christmas carol "We Three Kings." Make up a four-part short story on the lines below. For each king write about the country he may have come from and how he began his journey. Then write about what may have happened to bring them all together in their search.

KING #1: _____
_____
_____
_____
_____

KING #2: _____
_____
_____
_____
_____
_____

KING #3: _____
_____
_____
_____
_____

HOW THEY MET: _____
_____
_____
_____
_____

CHRISTMAS GIFTS

"... they presented unto him gifts; gold, and frankincense, and myrrh." Matthew 2:11

To: Grandma From: Tommy

To: Mom From: Max

Bible

OBJECTIVE: To encourage children to think of the needs of others at Christmastime.

MATERIALS: Construction paper, scissors, gift ribbon and holiday gift tags, large pattern of wise man, red background paper

PROCEDURE: Cover the bulletin board with red paper. Attach the enlarged pattern of the wise man and the appropriate lettering. After discussing the gifts the wise men brought to Jesus, ask the children to think of important gifts that others need. Conduct a class discussion about the needs of others, and ask each student to draw a picture of something he would like to give someone. After coloring and cutting out the picture, have the student attach a gift tag with the name of the person (or group of people) to receive the gift. Attach all the pictures of gifts to the bulletin board for all to share and enjoy. A class discussion can follow the completion of the bulletin board.

WISE MEN'S CAMEL MAZE

The search for Baby Jesus may have seemed like a long maze to the wise men. Can you find the path through this maze?

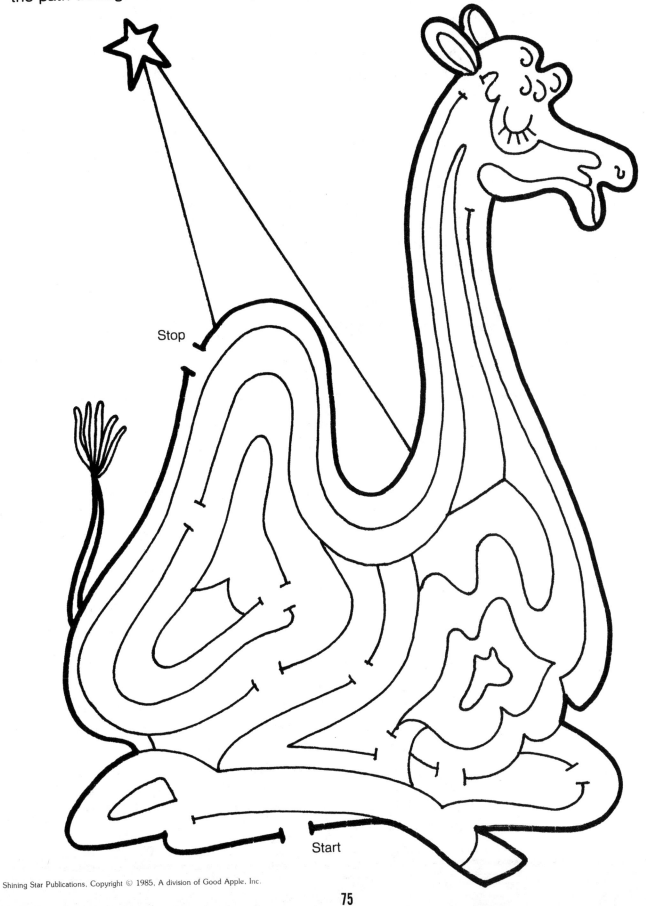

Stop

Start

GIFTS OF THE MAGI

Special gifts given at Christmastime commemorate the very first Christmas gifts given to the Christ Child by the wise men.

We can make our Christmas gifts even more special by creating special Christmas wrap of our own. The more thought we put into the WAY we give our gift, the more LOVE is shown to the person to whom we give our gift.

SPECIAL WRAPS

MATERIALS: Boxes and coffee cans, cotton balls (optional), scissors, glue, tape, wrapping paper, ribbon, yarn, construction paper, dowel rods or pencils for drumsticks.

PREPARATION: SANTA: Gift wrap a box in red paper. Glue a strip of black construction paper one-third the way from the bottom for Santa's belt. Cut an oval from pink or tan construction paper for a face. Use white paper or cotton balls for beard and eyebrows. Eyes, nose, moustache and mouth can be cut from construction paper. Santa's hat is made from red and white paper. TOY DRUM: Put your present inside a coffee can and replace the lid. Wrap the sides in holiday wrap. Zigzag colored yarn around the can, taping at top and bottom. Cover the top and bottom with strips of colored paper. Drumsticks are dowels or pencils with cut circles taped to ends.

CROWN HEADPIECES

Distribute dittoed or pre-cut STARS of various sizes to children. The children may color or decorate them with glitter, paint, scraps of fancy material or trim. The stars can then be cut out and glued onto sturdier cardboard.

For each headband, fold a 2-inch strip of construction paper in half to form a 1-inch strip. Staple the decorated stars to the center portion of each headband and then fit a headband to the head of each child.

MACARONI MOSAIC

DIRECTIONS:
1. Draw a large crown on a piece of construction paper or light cardboard. A crown pattern has been provided for you to copy, if you would like, on page 78.
2. Glue macaroni shapes to the crown. These shapes will represent valuable diamonds, rubies and emeralds.
3. Use a can of silver or gold spray paint to color your crown.
4. Cut out the crown after the paint dries.
5. Cut out a small headband and attach this to the crown. Now you can wear your crown!

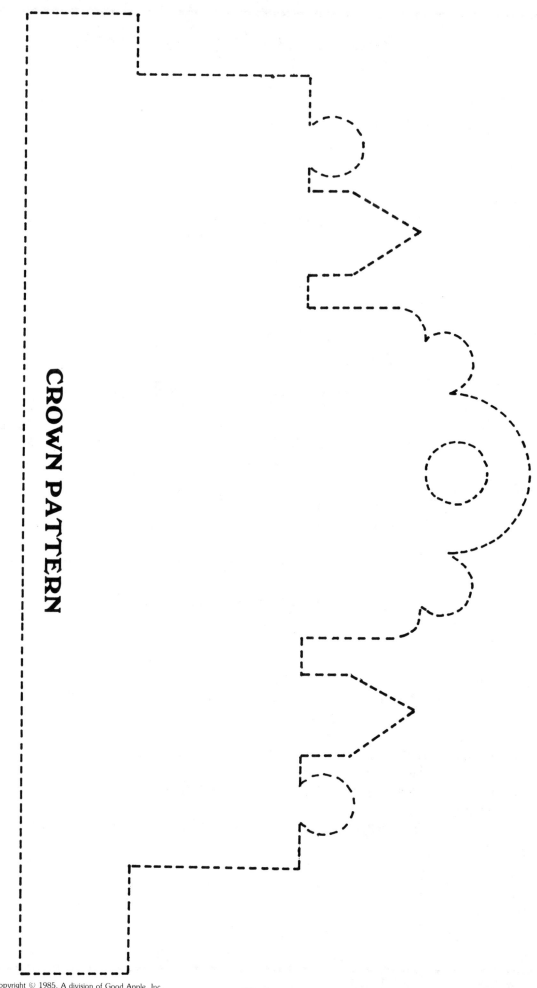

CROWN PATTERN

THE BABY JESUS

''And the child grew, and waxed strong in spirit, filled with wisdom: and the grace of God was upon him.'' (Luke 2:40) ''And Jesus increased in wisdom and stature, and in favour with God and man.'' (Luke 2:52)

We know so very little about the infancy and childhood of the Lord Jesus Christ. But the little that the Gospel writers do tell us about Baby Jesus and the boy Jesus lead us to believe that He was a leader among men even then, destined to lead the world in the way of light and truth.

Christmastime is the perfect time to learn and review the life and teachings of Jesus. Remembering our Savior and all that He has given the world is the best way to keep our Christmas a joyous and sacred celebration!

Jesus taught us many things and often in a very few words. See if you can find some Scriptures that teach us great lessons in a very few words. (Using red-letter editions of the Bible will help find Jesus' words quickly.)

Write some of your favorite teachings from Jesus and the Scriptures where you found them.

SHOWING LOVE FOR JESUS

If we want to show love for Jesus, we must follow Him. He said, ''If ye love me, keep my commandments.'' (John 14:15) This is an important commandment. Tell what you can do to keep the commandment Jesus has given us in this message.

THAT WONDERFUL NIGHT

A Choral Reading for Primary Grades
by Anna-Carolyn Gilbo, Hillsborough, NC

Announcer:
Once, long ago, there lived a man named Joseph and a woman named Mary. They were very happy because Mary was going to have a baby soon.

Chorus:
Joy, joy
On the way,
Joy, joy
Christmas Day.

Announcer:
Joseph and Mary had to go on a long trip to Bethlehem. They traveled very slowly. Joseph got a donkey for Mary to ride so that she would not have to walk such a long way.

Chorus:
Ride, ride
Night and day,
Ride, ride
Far away.

Announcer:
They were tired when they reached Bethlehem. They stopped, and Joseph asked, ''Do you have room for us?'' The man said he was sorry, but many people had come to Bethlehem, and he had no room for Joseph and Mary.

Chorus:
Tired, tired
There's no bed,
Tired, tired
Rest your head.

Announcer:
''My wife is very tired and needs a place to rest,'' Joseph said. ''Is there any place we can stay?'' The man took them to a barn where he kept his cows and sheep and all his animals. It was warm and dry there, and the hay smelled sweet and clean. Joseph smiled, ''This will be good. Thank you for your kindness.''

Chorus:
Rest, rest
We are here,
Rest, rest
Mary, dear.

Announcer:
That night Baby Jesus was born in the stable. Mary wrapped Him in soft, warm clothes and gently sang Him to sleep.

Chorus:
Sleep, sleep
Baby small
Sleep, sleep
On the straw.

words and music by Anna-Carolyn Gilbo

*Optional: Chorus may be sung using this melody. Accompaniment below.

(joyfully) Joy, joy On the way, Joy, joy Christ-mas Day.
(heavily) Ride, ride Night and day, Ride, ride Far a-way.
(slowly) Tired, tired There's no bed, Tired, tired Rest your head.
(gently) Rest, rest We are here, Rest, rest Mar-y dear.
(lullaby) Sleep, sleep Ba-by small, Sleep, sleep On the straw.
(quickly) Run, run Hur-ry now, Run, run You know how.
(brightly) Sing, sing An-gels bright, Sing, sing In the night.
(loudly) Love, love Je-sus small, Love, love To us all.

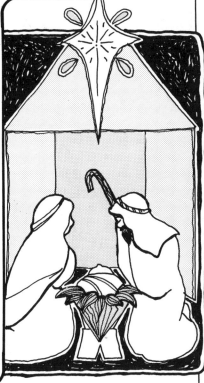

Announcer:
In a field near the barn, there were some shepherds taking care of their sheep. The sky began to glow brightly, and a beautiful angel said to them, "Do not be afraid."

Chorus:
Run, run
Hurry now,
Run, run
You know how.

Announcer:
Suddenly the sky was filled with angels. They sang a joyful song of love.

Chorus:
Sing, sing
Angels bright,
Sing, sing
In the night.

Announcer:
When the angels had gone, the shepherds said to each other, "Let's go find the baby." So they hurried to the barn. How happy they felt when they saw Mary, Joseph and Baby Jesus. They hurried to tell their friends all the things they had seen on this very wonderful night.

Chorus:
Love, love
Jesus small,
Love, love
To us all.

THE THINGS JESUS TAUGHT US

Words and Music by
Kathy Jones

FINISH THE LIST

The song "The Things Jesus Taught Us" mentions several things that Jesus taught us: love, forgiveness, helping one another, telling the truth, etc. Challenge the class to "finish the list." Start a large scroll and see how long it can get by listing all the things Jesus taught us. Each week let the class add more items. Be sure they include Scriptural references to back up their contributions. You may have to start a second scroll!!

2. Love all God's children.
3. Tell the truth

DRAW YOUR FAVORITE PARABLE

Jesus was the Master Teacher and often taught through parables. Some of them are listed below. Read the ones you are not familiar with and then pick your favorite one. Depict it in a picture or series of pictures (comic-strip fashion). Use the roller box idea for your pictures found on page 71.

My Favorite Parable is:

The Tares	The Good Samaritan
The Pearl of Great Price	The Lost Piece of Silver
The Ten Virgins	The Prodigal Son
The Talents	The Two Debtors

The first four parables are found in Matthew; the last four are found in Luke.

BE A SECOND MILER

Read Matthew 5:41. What does it mean for us today? What does the song mean when it says "Go the extra mile"? Draw a road map and show what you can do the first mile that would be nice. Then show what it would take to make your nice deed even nicer by going the extra mile. For example, helping your mother set the table would be going the first mile. Doing the dishes might make you a second miler. Washing the car for your dad is a good deed. Cleaning up the mess afterwards is something that makes the deed even nicer.

NAME POSTERS

The most important part of Christmas is the fact that JESUS was born. He came into the world because of God's great love for all of us. Here is another way to keep JESUS in the center of our Christmas celebration.

Make a giant name poster with the name JESUS in bold letters. You may use the patterns on pages 86 and 87 or use a style of your own. Put your letters on butcher paper, poster board or some other large paper—any size is fine, but the bigger the better. Fill in the letters with pictures and words that come to mind about Jesus' life: His birth, His teachings, events in His life. Make the poster colorful and display it somewhere in your church, class or home to help you remember who is at the CENTER of your Christmas season.

YOU are important to Jesus just as He is important to you. Now make your very own name poster all about you! What are your preferences, your favorite people, places, and things? Make a terrific poster for your room, your parents, your grandparents, for an open house or to share with your classmates! Now fill in the letters with ideas, drawings, photographs and other things that interest you personally. Give your poster added eye appeal by using crayons, markers, magazine pictures and lettering, colored chalk, and more.

FOLLOW HIS TEACHINGS

Sometimes there are lots of obstacles placed before us when we try to follow Jesus' teachings. See if you can get by them all on your way to a HAPPY LIFE.

Use the gameboard on the next page to demonstrate how difficult it may be to make progress if too many obstacles fall in our paths and how much help it is to have guideposts by which to travel.

Students flip a coin; heads move ahead two and tails move ahead three. When the child lands on an obstacle space, he or she names the obstacle and gives an example of a real-life situation that shows how the obstacle can become a pitfall. Then the player moves his or her marker back one space and passes the coin to the next player. If a player lands on a guidepost space, he or she gives a real-life situation that illustrates how this quality can lead to a happier life. Then the player moves one space forward before passing the coin to the next player. The game continues until one player reaches HOME. To avoid competition, have the children continue playing until all the players have reached HOME. Encourage the children to make their own gameboards using new obstacles and guideposts.

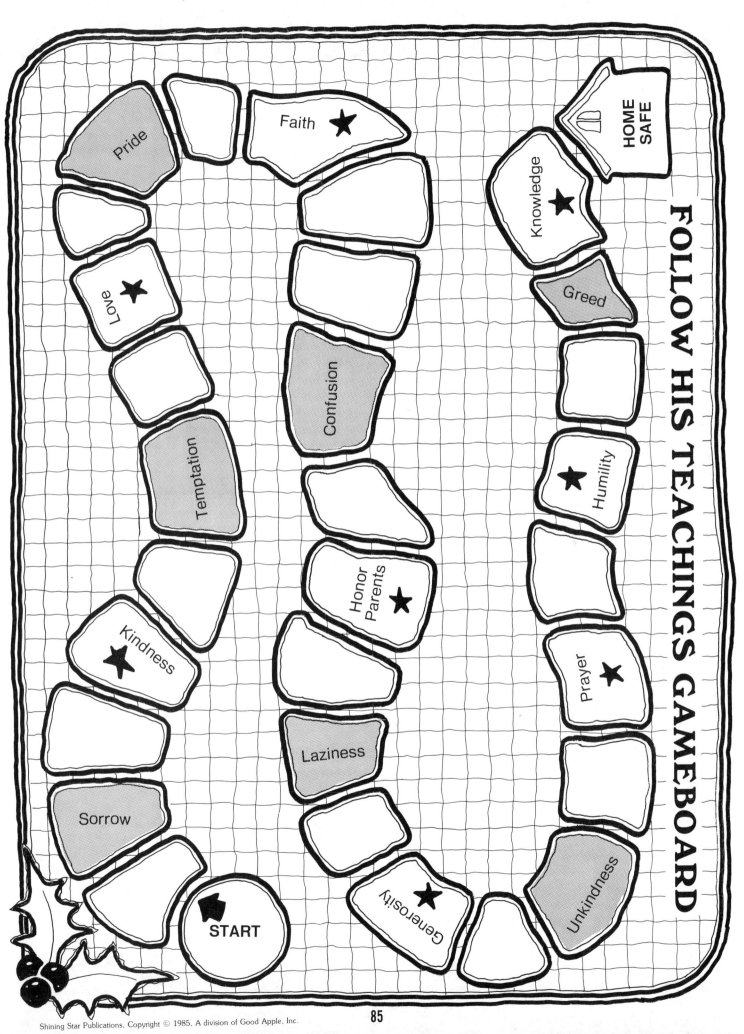

FOLLOW HIS TEACHINGS GAMEBOARD

Pride

Faith ★

Love ★

Temptation

Kindness ★

Sorrow

START

Confusion

Honor Parents ★

Laziness

Generosity ★

Unkindness

HOME SAFE

Knowledge ★

Greed

Humility ★

Prayer ★

85

Shining Star Publications, Copyright © 1985, A division of Good Apple, Inc.

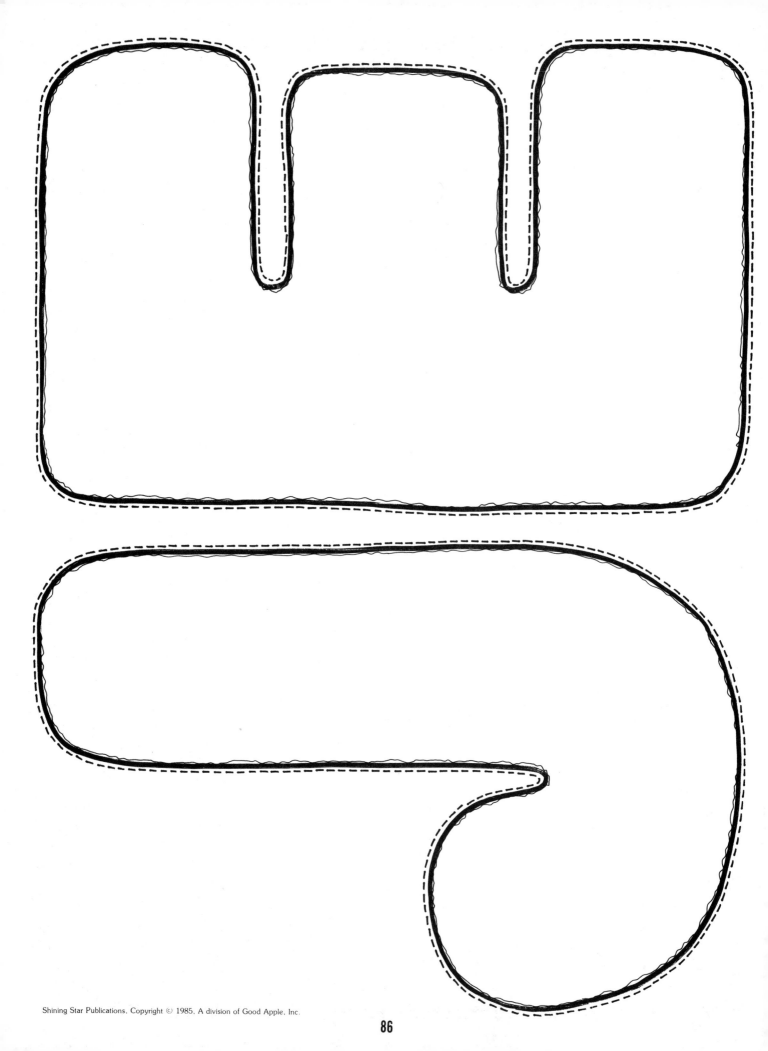

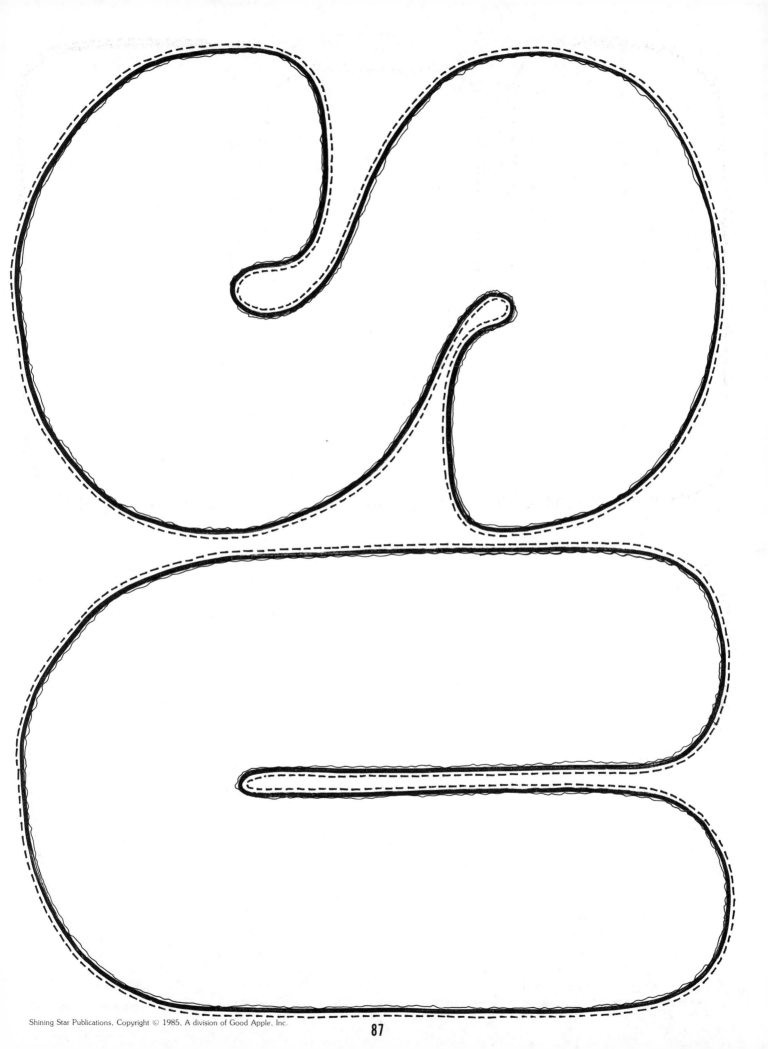

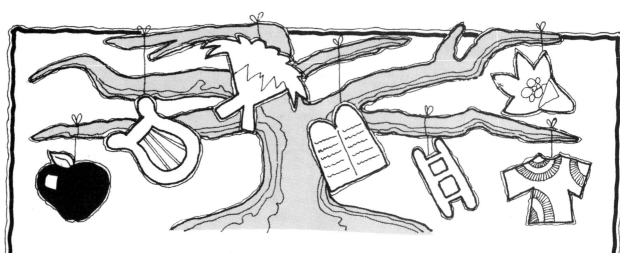

THE JESSE TREE

The Jesse Tree is an old custom which depicts the genealogy of Jesus Christ. Jesse was the father of King David, an early ancestor of Jesus. The idea of the tree is to create symbols which represent important people from Old and New Testaments, leading up to the birth of Jesus.

The Jesse Tree can be a real tree or one made from brown construction paper. The symbols can be made of fabric or paper. On the tree are some suggested symbols for you to use. Can you guess for whom each symbol stands? Can you give a Scripture reference for each? Answers can be found on page 144.

SYMBOLS OF BELONGING: Symbols have been used throughout history to show identity with families or groups. Can you think of some symbols that can be worn and/or displayed by those who wish to identify that they belong to a ''spiritual'' family, the family of JESUS?

Examples:

A cross symbolizes the fact that Jesus Christ died for our sins.
A crown symbolizes that Jesus is King of Kings.
A heart symbolizes love.
A dove symbolizes peace.

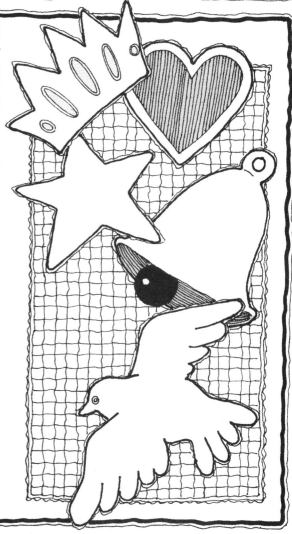

A bell _____

A star _____

A Bible _____

A Christian flag_____

A church _____

Think of some other symbols that you identify with a special part of Christmas or Christ's birth. Design an armband or patch that you and your family members or classmates could wear to remind you of this special part of celebrating Christmas.

FAMILIES: GOD'S SPECIAL GIFT TO US

"... and when the parents brought in the child Jesus ... Joseph and his mother marvelled at those things which were spoken of him." Luke 2:27, 33

Joseph, Mary and the Christ Child are the First Family of Christmas, a very special family indeed. Christmas is a most important time for remembering one of the greatest gifts God has given all of us: FAMILY. The more we learn about Christ and HIS family, the First Family of Christmas, the happier we can make our OWN families as we celebrate the joys of the Christmas season together.

CHRISTMAS PLACE MATS

MATERIALS:
12'' X 18'' red and green construction paper
permanent felt-tipped marking pens (black and assorted colors) with tips of varying widths
clear Con-Tact paper

DIRECTIONS:
Create a Christmas place mat for each member of your family. Divide a sheet of red or green construction paper into sections. Use a black, felt-tipped permanent marking pen to outline these sections. Think about all the things you like about each member of your family. Illustrate each of these things in a different section of the mat. When all the spaces have been filled in and colored, cover your mat with clear Con-Tact paper. Use the mats for Christmas dinner or any time of the year!

MY HOME
by Kathy Jones

1. Long a - go and some - where far a - way;
2. Some - day soon or ma - ny years from now,

had a home; 'Twas the glo - ri - ous, they say.

Trail - ing clouds of glo - ry, As the po - et said,
Through a veil of mem - ories, Home - ward bound I'll fly,

Came we here to earth to learn, By faith and know - ledge led
To that place so long a - go,

To a Fath - er that I know, To a Light that

in me glows, To His man - sion high.

MY HOME AND FAMILY

The family into which Jesus was born was special indeed. From the time of His birth until manhood, Jesus did all He could to make that home a heaven on earth. Here are some ways to help make our families like that of Joseph, Mary, and Jesus—the First Family of Christmas.

My Home in Heaven

MAKING A HEAVENLY HOME

My Home on Earth

Read John 14:2 and talk about what you think Jesus meant by "many mansions." What does the song "My Home" mean by "His mansion high"? Draw on paper two homes (simple outlines) or construct them by using pieces of cardboard pasted or taped together. Label one "My Home on Earth" and the other "My Home in Heaven." Paste strips of paper on each with descriptions of what you think the first **is** like and what you think the other **will be** like. Now draw (or construct) a bridge between the two homes. From the bridge, hang ideas you have that will help make your home on earth more like your home in heaven.

Example: Home on earth—noisy, too loud sometimes
Home in heaven—serene, always peaceful
Idea to bridge the gap—play lovely, quiet music more often

BECAUSE ALL MEN ARE BROTHERS

Romans 8:16 and Ephesians 4:6 remind us that we all have one Father. Write a short story about a boy or girl who does not understand that we are all brothers and sisters but whose behavior towards other people changes when something happens to make him/her realize this. Share your story.

THE LIGHT WITHIN US

MY FAITH

Read Acts 17:28 and the line from the song "My Home" that says "To a Light that in me glows." What do they mean? There is a little bit of God in all of us; we are His children. How can we make the Light that is in us glow more brightly?
Light a candle. Have the students think of all the ways the candle can be put out and list them. Then have them think of all the ways the candle can be made to last longer and glow more brightly. Prepare work sheets with a candle at the top of each page and the words **MY FAITH** inscribed on it. Make two columns beneath the candle, one for listing ways the student's candle could be put out and the other for ways the student's candle could be made to glow more brightly.

Sometimes being a wonderful family member is kind of difficult. Christmastime is a special time for families and a time for being extra kind to one another. **But what about the day after Christmas?**

This page may help us to be more like the First Family of Christmas **AFTER** Christmas as well as before and during.

THE DAY AFTER CHRISTMAS

by Alice Bach

Harper & Row, 1975

Alice Bach has created a simple, whimsical story that deals rather nonchalantly with children's attitudes about themselves and life in general. Though not deeply thought-provoking, the plight of Emily the day after Christmas is one with which most children will readily identify, whether admittedly or not. The post-Christmas season is a good time for children to make an extra effort to fight that inevitable letdown feeling, recount their blessings, and take a fresh look at God's beautiful creations.

Follow-up: ''. . . be of good cheer . . . .'' (John 16:33)
Materials: Note pads, pencils, drawing paper, crayons or watercolors.
Activity: Following the Christmas season, we all sometimes feel a bit letdown. This is a good time for the children to remember all the things they have to ''be of good cheer'' about. Read John 16:33 together. Remind the class of the circumstances in which Jesus said those words—shortly before the events in Gethsemane and on Calvary. If He could still say ''be of good cheer,'' all of us can find things to be cheerful about, too, even after Christmas is over. Go on a walking field trip for several blocks, and have the children list on note pads all the beautiful things for which we should be grateful and happy. Don't forget our bodies: eyes, ears, legs, arms, etc. Return to class or home and share lists. Then have each child make a drawing or painting of one or two items he listed that make him cheerful about life. Challenge the class to think about their lists whenever they feel ''down.''

HE KNOWS US ALL

The Lord knows us better than we know ourselves. He knew Jeremiah before he was born (Jeremiah 1:5) as He knew each of us before we were born (Ephesians 1:4). See how well you know each other. Write down on a piece of paper something you think no one else knows about you (and that you wouldn't mind sharing, of course). Have everyone place his paper in a hat or box. Take turns drawing and reading aloud. See who knows whom the best. Remember: God knows us all better than anyone, even ourselves.

WE ARE FAMILY

Make a shadow box depicting all the members of your family. Use a shoe box turned on its side. Paint it inside and out, or cover it with wrapping paper, Con-Tact paper, or foil. Make the family members out of pipe cleaners, and position them around tables and chairs made from matchboxes, Popsicle sticks, thimbles, buttons, etc. Glue all in place. Proudly display your **FAMILY** at home and share with friends and relatives who visit you.

WE NEED EACH OTHER

During the next week, have each person in your family write a letter to every other family member telling him or her why he or she is needed. This will encourage each person to think seriously about what the other family members mean in his life. It will also give a boost to all of you to know that you are needed and why. Remember, though, that knowing what needs you fill for the members of your family is likely to make clear the responsibilities you have to them, too!

Shining Star Publications, Copyright © 1985, A division of Good Apple, Inc.

CHRISTMAS IS A TIME FOR SHARING

What would Christmas be like without family and friends with whom to celebrate?

Using the wreath below, picture all the loved ones with whom you plan to share the blessings of the Christmas season.

On the next page, use the cutout pictures or make pictures of your own to show who wanted to share the first Christmas with Baby Jesus and His family: shepherds, angels, animals, wise men. Color or paint each cameo picture, cut out, and glue onto your wreath.

Cut out both wreaths, paste to cardboard, and decorate with real bows! Now share your pictures with someone!

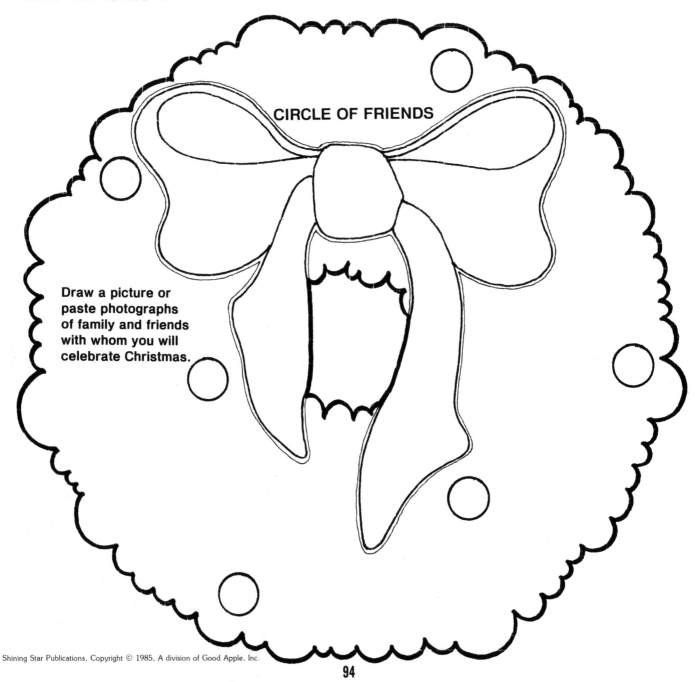

CIRCLE OF FRIENDS

Draw a picture or
paste photographs
of family and friends
with whom you will
celebrate Christmas.

THE FIRST CHRISTMAS WAS A TIME FOR SHARING

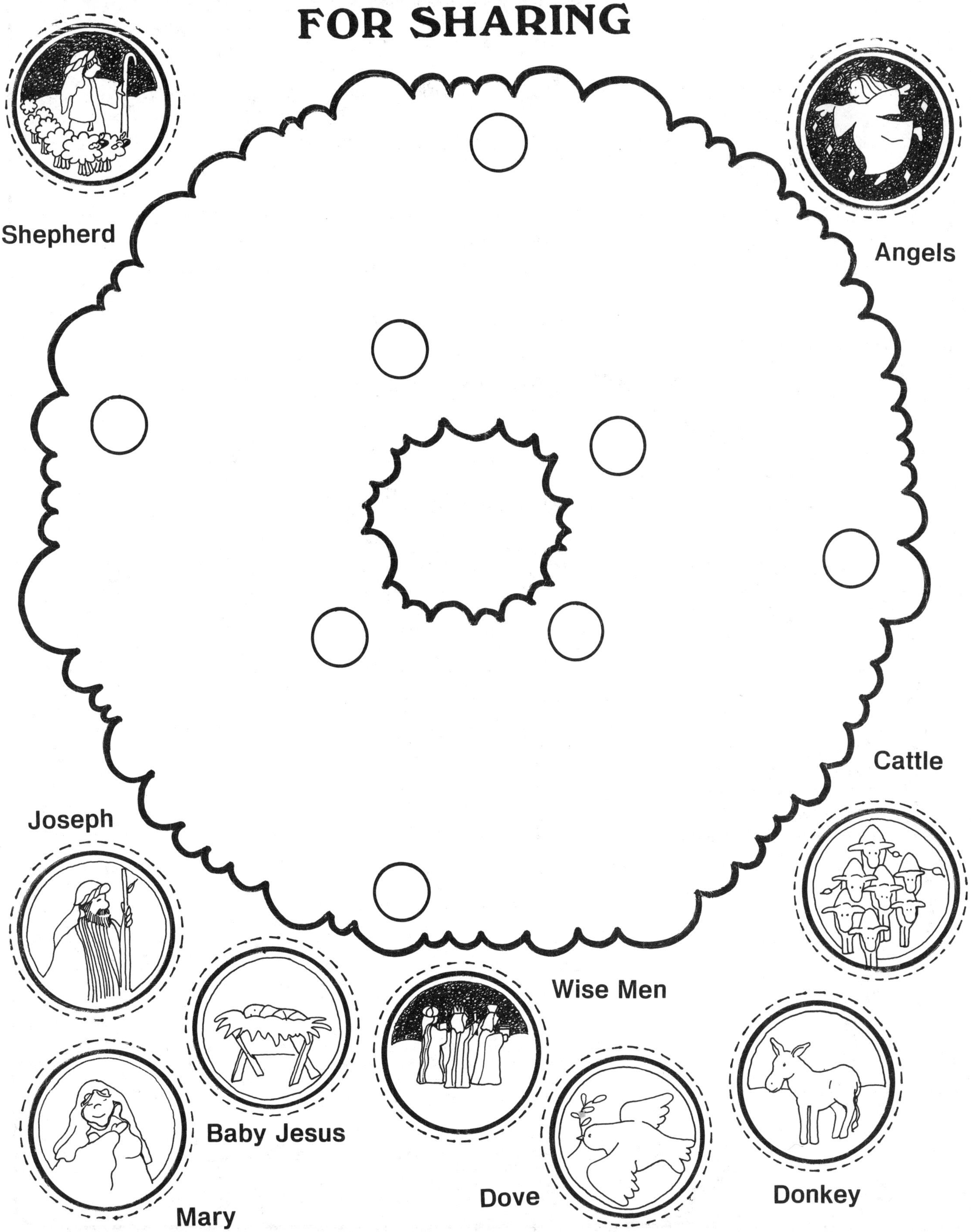

Shepherd

Angels

Cattle

Joseph

Wise Men

Baby Jesus

Dove

Donkey

Mary

THERE IS NO OTHER

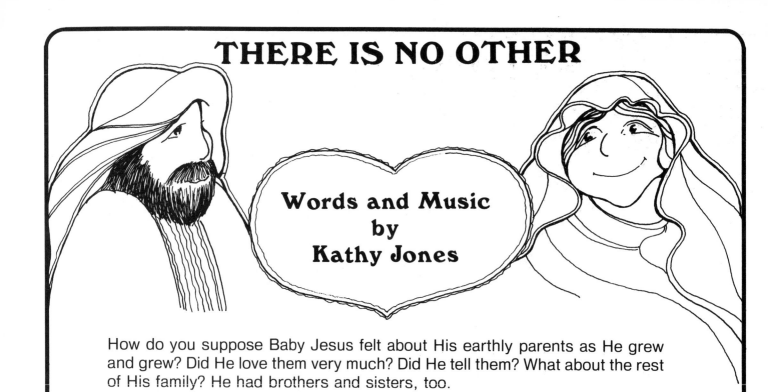

Words and Music by Kathy Jones

How do you suppose Baby Jesus felt about His earthly parents as He grew and grew? Did He love them very much? Did He tell them? What about the rest of His family? He had brothers and sisters, too.

Sing this song and think about how little Lord Jesus felt about His family. The following pages will help us CELEBRATE CHRISTMAS a little better by remembering to LOVE OUR FAMILIES.

1. There is no oth-er like my moth-er; She's the best I
2. There is no oth-er like my fath-er; He can make me

know. There is no oth-er like my moth-er; And I love her
glad. There is no oth-er like my fath-er; I sure love my

so.
dad.

Verse 3. There is no other like my brother;
He's a friend to me.
There is no other like my brother;
We are family.

Verse 4. There is no other like my sister;
She helps me each day.
There is no other like my sister;
I think she's okay.

HE'S A FRIEND TO ME

There is no other like my brother. He's a friend to me. Think of all the ways your brother helps you. Choose five of these ways, print them on a bookmark, poster or award, and present it to your brother. If you have more than one brother, you will have to make several awards. If you appreciate your brother and you know it, let him know it, too!

HAPPY HELPERS

There is no other like a helpful sister! If you are someone's sister, think of all the ways you can be a happy helper at home, especially to your brother or sister or both! Draw a picture of your brother or sister and think of five ways you plan to help him or her this week. Ask your mother or teacher to list these ways on the back of your picture. Put a star by each one after you've been a helpful sister.

1.

2.

3.

4.

5.

THE CHRISTMAS FAMILY COLOR GAME

Christmas is one of the most colorful times of year! Not just red and green, but nearly every color of the rainbow seems to be used in decorating homes, schools, churches, neighborhoods. Colors of all sorts add a festive touch to our gifts, our trees, even our food. The burst of color we see at Christmastime reminds us of the great joy we all feel at the celebration of the birth of our Savior!

Celebrate Christmas with your family or friends by playing the Christmas Family Color Game.

PREPARATION: Obtain a spinner or one die. Cut out the markers below and glue them onto sturdy cardboard. Color the spaces on the gameboard on the following page that are marked with a color name. Read the rules and you're ready!

RULES: All spin or throw the die once to determine which player goes first. Then take turns in a clockwise direction, passing the spinner or die to the person on your left.

Follow the directions on the **word** spaces, and move ahead or back as indicated. A space marked with a star is a free spin.

If you land on a **color** space, you have 10 seconds to find something in your home or class that is that color. The other players can use a second hand on a watch or clock or count slowly to 10. If you find something with the right color, you move ahead two spaces and then pass your turn. If you can find **two** things of the right color, you move ahead three spaces.

The first player to reach the Christmas tree wins! You do not need an exact number to reach the tree.

MARKERS:

START

Helped Mom. Move ahead 2.

Red

Quarrelled with Dad. Go back 3.

Blue

Took cookies to a neighbor. Move ahead 2.

Pink

Green

Orange

Yellow

Forgot to say thank you. Go back 2.

Brown

Forgot to brush teeth. Go back 2.

Black

Silver

White

Purple

Green

Pink

Memorized a Bible verse. Take a free turn.

Picked up toys. Go ahead 3.

Pink

Red

Green

WE'RE VERY GOOD FRIENDS, MY BROTHER AND I

Written and Illustrated by P.K. Hallinan
Children's Press, 1973

This lyrical book is written in a poetic form that will delight and charm all readers. Enhanced by the comical and often touching illustrations, P.K. Hallinan's book lovingly touches on some poignant moments in childhood, especially on family ties and the relationship to loved ones. This simplistic yet ever so sensitive work is a winner for everyone who reads it.

Follow-up: "He that loveth his brother . . . ." (I John 2:10)

Materials: Mural paper (plain shelf paper will do), watercolors or crayons, felt markers, lined paper and pencils

Activity: Discuss what the Lord meant when He talked about loving our brother. Did He only mean brothers in our family? Who is our "brother" then? Have the children make two lists. On the first, they are to write the names of all the people they consider friends. On the second, they are to write the names of those they love. From their lists, make a double mural (one on top of the other) with each child drawing a picture of a friend on one and someone he/she loves on the other. Under each figure, the child could write one reason why that person is his/her friend or loved one. Then compare lists, pictures, reasons for love and friendship. Help the class discover that the people we love are really our friends, too, and that our friends are also people we love.

MY BROTHER AND I

Read aloud the book entitled *We're Very Good Friends, My Brother and I* by P.K. Hallinan. Brothers can be such great friends if we let them. Role play a situation where friends want you to go somewhere with them but you choose to stay and play with your brother as planned. Show how happy this makes him. Make up other situations that show how you and your brother can be friends, and role play each one. (This activity works great for sisters, too.)

Make an award for your brother, sister, mother, dad or some other member of your family. Present it to him or her at a special time, such as family night or during private prayer time. Let him or her know what the award is for and throw in a big kiss and hug!!!

GIFTS

'' . . . and when they had opened their treasures, they presented unto him gifts; gold, and frankincense, and myrrh.''

Matthew 2:11

God gave us all the very first Christmas gift when He gave us Baby Jesus, the Savior of the world. The wise men gave the next Christmas gifts when they brought their treasures and laid them before the infant King.

That first Christmas an important tradition began, giving gifts to one another to commemorate the giving of God's greatest gift of all!

'' . . . God so loved the world, that he gave his only begotten Son, that whosoever believeth in him should not perish, but have everlasting life.''

John 3:16

Before you make your Christmas gift list, fill out this gift list from God of all the gifts you already have! Do it as a class and watch the list grow and grow. The list could go on forever.

Gifts

"GIFTS FROM GOD" BULLETIN BOARD

Fold different sizes of construction paper in half. Decorate one side of paper as a gift box. Be sure to include a gift tag, such as "To Mary, from God." (Use all the children's names on packages.) On the inside, paste a picture of a gift from God and an appropriate Bible verse. (Verses included in this book and from the creation story in Genesis 1 will help you.) Position finished "gifts" under a large Christmas tree. Staple them so the decorated sides may be lifted to reveal the pictures and verses.

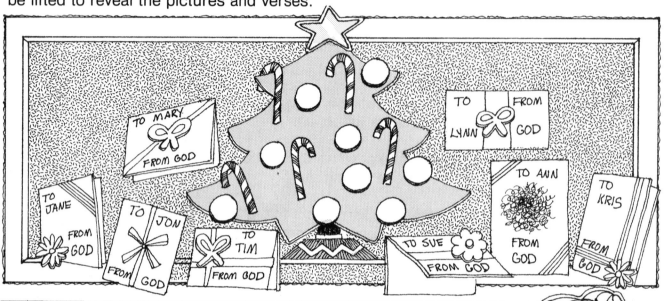

A GIFT OF SELF

A PHONE CALL A DAY

Set aside a small amount of time every day to give a phone call to someone for whom that small piece of time may be the brightest spot of the day! This "someone" may be a relative, a lonely neighbor, an older person who lives alone, or someone sick. Give a call at the same time every day just to say "Hi! How are you?" or "Are you okay?" or "We're thinking of you" or "Is there anything you need?" Keep that person in touch with the outside world by telling some interesting or informative bits of news. Each member of your family can be a caller to a separate person. Just think of what it will mean to some person to KNOW that at least one other human being cares enough to call every day. In some cases, your call may be important in giving help that otherwise no one would know was needed!

Memorize John 3:16.

GOD'S GIFT OF SALVATION

''For God so loved the world, that he gave his only begotten Son, that whosoever believeth in him should not perish, but have everlasting life.'' John 3:16

Use the following movements with this verse:

God - arms extended to heaven, head tilted back to look to heaven

world - hands outline circle (globe)

gave - hands extended outward from chest; palms up ''to give''

only Son - point to nail marks of Christ; first in one palm, then the other

whosoever - hand sweeps all in room

believeth - point to brain

not - hands crossed, palms down, bring hands to sides with sharp motion

perish - let head drop

everlasting - smile, arms outstretched to heaven

CHRISTMAS CARD BOOKMARK

Cut a cross shape out of an old Christmas card. Punch a hole in the top. Add a 6-inch yarn tie. Write a Bible verse referring to God's gift of salvation on the back. Be sure to include the Scripture reference.

GIFT TREE

Cut out gift boxes that the children can decorate and attach to a tree for classroom decorations. (See pattern on next page.) Have each child write on his gift box a gift he has received from God or one he plans to GIVE BACK TO GOD for Christmas this year.

To make a tree: Put a bare branch through the hole of an inverted flower pot. A glob of clay may be put at the end of the branch to anchor it inside the pot.

GIFT BOX
PATTERN
(See page 103.)

WAX PAPER
WINDOW
HANGING

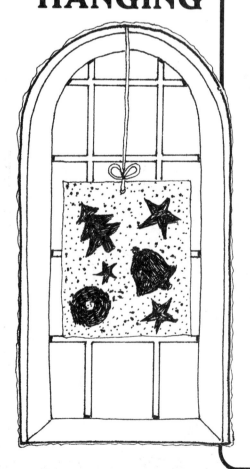

Here's another Christmas project! It's a beautiful Christmas gift that can be hung near a window to remind others of the special and wonderful star of Bethlehem that led the wise men to Jesus.

Materials:
1. black construction paper
2. wax paper
3. old crayons
4. table knives and scissors
5. iron
6. newspaper

Cut Christmas shapes (stars, trees, snowflakes, angels, etc.) from construction paper. These shapes will become a part of a Christmas hanging collage.

Next scrape bits of colored crayon onto an 18'' long piece of wax paper. Arrange the cutout shapes on the wax paper and place another sheet of wax paper on top of the first one.

Place the sheets between old newspaper, and use a hot iron to melt the wax paper and crayons together. The resulting collage can be hung on a window as a ''stained glass'' Christmas hanging.

GREAT GIFT IDEAS!

SNOW SCENES

. . . from a baby food jar

Materials:
Baby food jar, paint, glue, small piece of artificial pine tree, molding clay, moth crystals

Preparation:
An easy craft idea for the winter season is to make a snow scene in a baby food jar (especially nice at Christmas).

First, paint the lid of the baby food jar with gold enamel. Allow it to dry overnight.

Glue a small piece of artificial pine on the inside of the lid so when the lid lies upside down, the pine stands up like a tree. (Molding clay can be used to adhere tree to lid, also.) Put 1 teaspoon of moth crystals in the jar. Fill the jar with water. Put lid on jar. As the jar is turned over and back onto its lid again, snow falls into the pine tree.

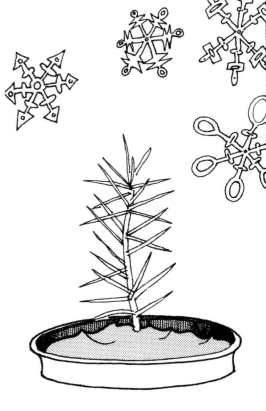

. . . from a paper plate

Materials:
19'' paper plate, 19'' x 12'' sheet of dark blue construction paper, white paint, yarn, rickrack, lace scraps, construction paper scraps, assorted colors, paintbrushes, glue, scissors, pencils

Preparation:
Trace the shape of the paper plate onto the blue construction paper and cut out.

Cut out the center of the paper plate to form a frame. Paint a snow scene on the blue construction paper circle. Point out that part of the circle will be covered by the "frame." Add color details from construction paper scraps.

Glue the frame to the snow scene, and trim with lace, yarn, etc.

BIBLICAL SPICE WREATH

Glue seeds on a styrofoam wreath. Separate each section with a broken toothpick. Decorate the side of the wreath with cloth tape or ribbon. Tie a ribbon on the top. Discuss the spices mentioned in the Bible and those used on the wreath. Some possible seeds to use are:

1. Sesame: yields an oil which was used for cooking in early Biblical history.
2. Flax: cultivated by Egyptians before the exodus. Flax was the only plant grown for cloth. (Exodus 9:31) Part of God's judgement was the taking away of the flax. (Hosea 2:9)
3. Split peas: possibly one of the vegetables Daniel requested, following Hebrew law, instead of eating the king's dainties and wine. (Deuteronomy 14:23; Daniel 1:16)
4. Rice: staple used by Christians and non-Christians for centuries.
5. Red lentils: Esau sold his birthright to Jacob for pottage. (Genesis 25:29-34)
6. Wheat: symbolic of the doctrine of resurrection. For example, wheat dies before it produces abundantly. (I Corinthians 15:35-38) Wheat was grown in Palestine in 700 B.C. and is known as ''the staff of life.''
7. Poppy seed: used medicinally.
8. Rosemary: Scripturally used to point out ostentation and hypocrisy of the Pharisees who tithed even the commonest of herbs. These shrubs are now grown in the Garden of Gethsemane.
9. Mustard: used by Christ as an illustration of something which develops rapidly from a small beginning, for example, the faith of an individual. (Mark 4:30-32)
10. Mung: crop used by earliest Palestinians.

MORE GIFT IDEAS

—FOR SOMEONE SPECIAL—

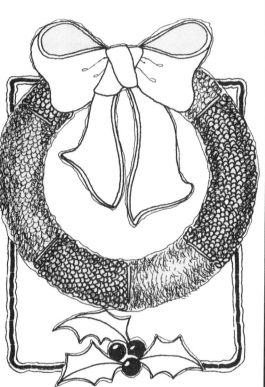

BALL ORNAMENT

Materials:
round balloon
string or yarn
laundry starch

Directions:
Blow balloon to desired size of ornament and tie. Mix laundry starch to medium thickness, or use liquid starch. (Starch may be tinted with food coloring if white string is used.) Dip the string or yarn into the starch, and wind around and around over the balloon. When the balloon is nearly covered with the string, hang it to dry overnight. When the starched string is dry, prick the balloon to let the air out. The stiff string covering will retain the shape of the balloon. This is a delicate ornament to hang in a doorway or about the room.

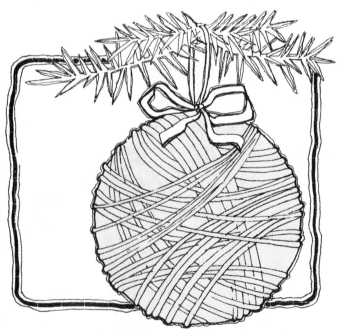

PAINTED PEANUT WREATH

Materials:
One 12-inch cardboard circle (this can be obtained from a bakery, pizza establishment, or a store that sells cake decorating materials), styrofoam pieces (collected from packages), green spray paint, red crepe paper for bow (2'' x 54''), glue, containers for glue

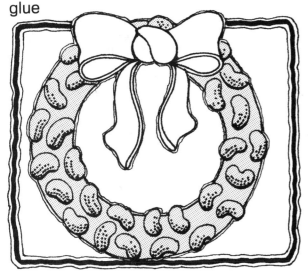

Preparation:
Using a sharp knife, cut a 6½-inch circle in the middle of a cardboard circle.

Show the children how to glue styrofoam curls to cardboard, placing them close together.

Provide a container filled with glue in which the children may dip their pieces.

Let dry overnight. Spray with green paint. Make a bow by cutting crepe paper 2 inches wide. If children are unable to tie bows, tie enough for the class. An alternative idea would be to wrap the bow around the entire piece and tie.

FUN WITH MACARONI

You can make interesting projects out of different shapes of macaroni.

Materials:
macaroni (many different shapes)
markers

Directions:
Color the macaroni with the markers. String them on yarn to make necklaces. This would be a great gift for Christmas!

COOKIE GIFT WRAP

Materials:
Tissue paper
Assorted metal cookie cutters
Paints
Aluminum pie tins or other flat containers for paint

Directions:
Dip cookie cutter into paint and press onto paper. Show students how to develop a ''pattern'' with simple repeats and how to create a ''random'' pattern effect.

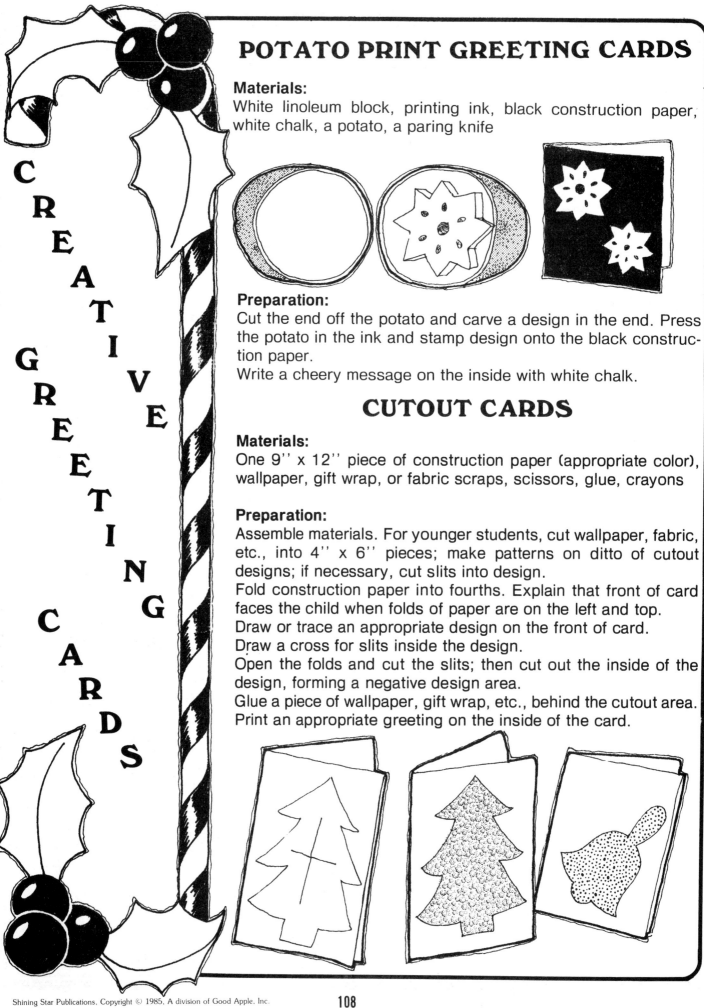

POTATO PRINT GREETING CARDS

Materials:
White linoleum block, printing ink, black construction paper, white chalk, a potato, a paring knife

Preparation:
Cut the end off the potato and carve a design in the end. Press the potato in the ink and stamp design onto the black construction paper.
Write a cheery message on the inside with white chalk.

CUTOUT CARDS

Materials:
One 9'' x 12'' piece of construction paper (appropriate color), wallpaper, gift wrap, or fabric scraps, scissors, glue, crayons

Preparation:
Assemble materials. For younger students, cut wallpaper, fabric, etc., into 4'' x 6'' pieces; make patterns on ditto of cutout designs; if necessary, cut slits into design.
Fold construction paper into fourths. Explain that front of card faces the child when folds of paper are on the left and top.
Draw or trace an appropriate design on the front of card.
Draw a cross for slits inside the design.
Open the folds and cut the slits; then cut out the inside of the design, forming a negative design area.
Glue a piece of wallpaper, gift wrap, etc., behind the cutout area.
Print an appropriate greeting on the inside of the card.

(vertical text) CREATIVE GREETING CARDS

QUICKIE CHRISTMAS CARD

Color the Christmas card. Cut it out and fold it on the dotted line. Cut **very carefully.** The envelope is on the reverse side.

''For God so loved the world . . . .''
John 3:16

Love to you at Christmas and always.

This card would make a nice gift for someone you love who is far away.

Address the envelope and sign your name. Color it. Fold it shut on the dotted line. Seal it with a Christmas seal and send it to a friend.

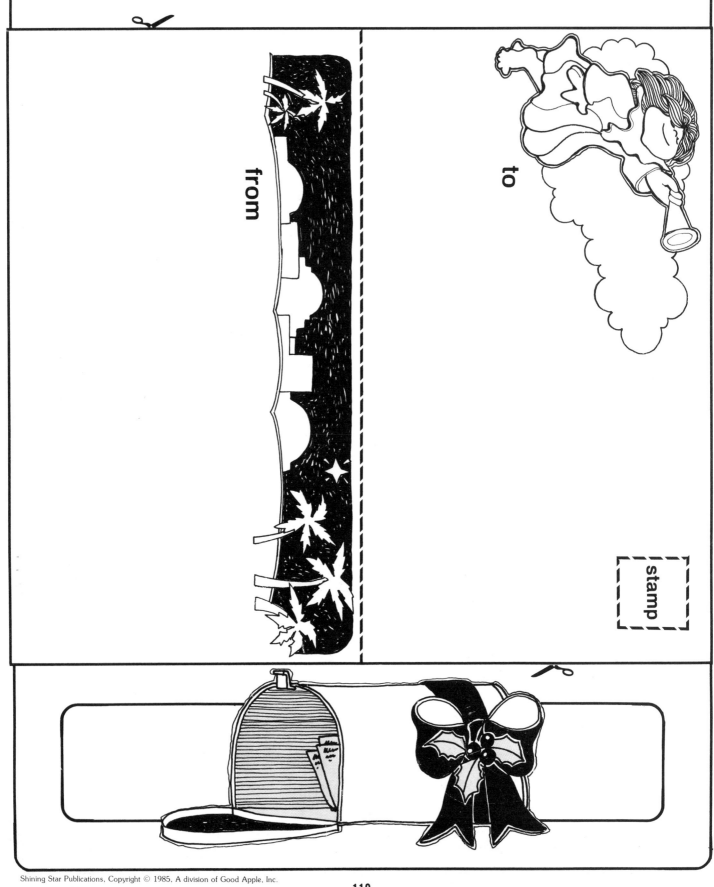

from

to

stamp

HOLIDAY GIFT TAGS (front)

Color the tags and cut them out carefully. Punch out the holes and tie them on your Christmas gifts. Write your "to . . . from . . ." message on the back of each tag.

HOLIDAY GIFT TAGS (back)

Cut out the tags very carefully and write your "to . . . from . . ." message very neatly. Color the backside of your gift tag.

to	from
○	

to	from
○	

to	from
○	

to	from
○	

to	from
○	

to	from
○	

to	from
○	

to	from
○	

to	from
○	

CHRISTMAS POTPOURRI

This section includes all the Christmas ODDS and ENDS ideas that can make the holiday season a little more fun. It also includes some ideas for making your Christmas pageant or play a little more special, whether you use the one included in this book or another. The job chart shown could be used for everyday assignments OR for special assignments during your play production (programs, invitations, usher, set designer, etc.). The angel napkin rings could be duplicated and used with refreshments served after your Christmas play.

HELPER CHART

HELPER CHART: The child's name should be attached by colored yarn to the job assignment using the same color as the BELL that carries his name.

ANGEL NAPKIN RINGS: Duplicate the angel pattern on heavy paper. Color the angel, cut out carefully, insert Tab A into Slot B, fold tab over and tape.

ANGEL NAPKIN RINGS

This bulletin board should have a light background (light blue, perhaps), and the large letters in the word JOY could be made from bright gift-wrap paper. Have the children discuss all the JOY that God brings to earth, not just at Christmas but all year through. In the center of the ''O,'' post a list of CLASSROOM JOYMAKERS that could include those students who bring the class JOY with their kindness, service, good behavior, super-efforts, etc. It could be each student's goal to make the JOYMAKER list before Christmas!

BULLETIN BOARD IDEAS

Aluminum foil or metallic paper could be used to make the bells in this Christmas bulletin board. Real extra-wide ribbon could be used for the bow and real evergreen branches could be used behind the bells OR construction paper branches and bow would be just fine. After Christmas, the caption could change to read ''RING OUT THE OLD, RING IN THE NEW'' with a class list of New Year's resolutions. Another caption might read ''WORK WORTH RINGING ABOUT'' with posted examples of exceptional classroom work.

CHRISTMAS WITHOUT THE SCRIPTURES . . .

would be like a day without Sunshine!

1 Luke 1:26,27	**2** Luke 1:28	**3** Luke 1:29	**4** Luke 1:30,31

5 Luke 1:32,33	**6** Luke 1:34,35	**7** Luke 1:36	**8** Luke 1:37	**9** Luke 1:38	**10** Luke 1:39
11 Luke 1:40,41	**12** Luke 1:42	**13** Luke 1:43	**14** Luke 1:44	**15** Luke 1:45	**16** Luke 1:46,47
17 Luke 1:48,49	**18** Luke 1:50,51	**19** Luke 1:52,53	**20** Luke 1:54-56	**21** Luke 2:1,2	**22** Luke 2:3,4
23 Luke 2:5	**24** Luke 2:6	**25** Luke 2:7-20	**26** Luke 2:21	**27** Luke 2:22	**28** Luke 2:23
29 Luke 2:24	**30** Luke 2:25,26	**31** Luke 2:27-33			

Each day in December, read the corresponding Scripture in Luke about the birth of Jesus. When you have read the verse/verses, color the appropriate sun.

CHRISTMAS ORNAMENTS

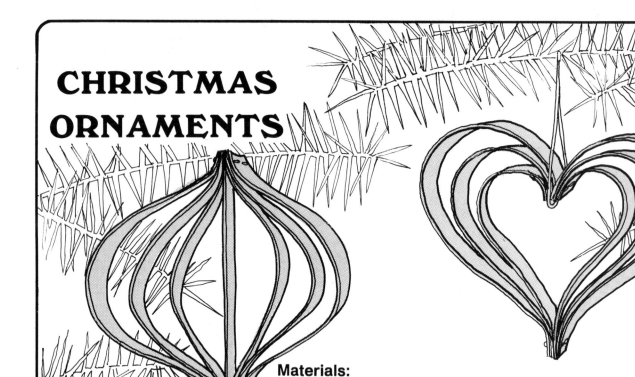

Materials:

Paper, scissors, stapler, thread

Preparation:

These three ornaments pictured above are all made from paper strips stapled together and hung from thread. For the three rings, cut three strips ¾'' wide, in 3 lengths: 18'', 15'', and 12''.

For the upper left design, start with seven strips ¾'' wide. The center strip is 5½'' long, the inside two are 6'' long, the next two are 6½'' long, and the outside strips are 7'' long. For the heart cut six strips, each ½'' wide. The outside strips are 9'', the next two are 7½'', the inside two are 6''.

CHRISTMAS BALL

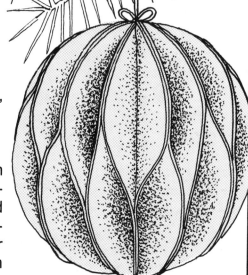

Materials:

Paper (a wallpaper book would provide great paper for this), scissors, glue, string, stapler

Preparation:

From the paper of your choice, cut 9 circles 5 inches in diameter. Fold each one in half and crease it through the middle. Open circles up, stack them on top of each other, and staple them on the crease in 3 places: top, middle, and bottom. Alternating top and bottom, glue the pieces together about ⅓ of the way to the center. Hang from a thread run through the top of the ornament.

CHRISTMAS IS A TIME TO BE TOGETHER

BIBLE STORY CUT-UPS

Use the imagination, energy and ingenuity of every family member to re-create a favorite Bible story with words, pictures and letters that you cut from magazines.

1. Gather your supplies: several old magazines or newspapers, scissors for each family member, glue, a large piece of poster board, a Bible.

2. Choose a favorite story from the Bible to retell. Review the story by telling it or reading it from the Bible. Agree on what words you'll need for telling the story.

3. Start cutting out words, letters and pictures that will become a part of the story. As you begin to re-create the story, lay out the words or pictures on the poster board. You may NOT use pen or pencil to write parts of words. You MAY piece together words by cutting out individual letters.

4. When you have the story ready, glue all the words in place on the poster board. Then read the story together.

STRAIGHT TALK

WORSHIP IDEA: The Bible gives Christians a plan for growing as God's children. Some of the plan includes very specific instructions for practical life situations.

DO TOGETHER:

1. Find the DOs and DON'Ts of these Bible passages.

2. As you find each instruction, write it down on a poster so that your family can keep these as part of a visible plan for behavior.

Ephesians 6:1	Ephesians 6:5
I Timothy 6:17	Luke 6:27
Matthew 5:5	Matthew 5:16
Ephesians 4:26	Ephesians 4:29
Ephesians 4:32	Luke 6:31
Romans 12:10	Romans 12:12
Romans 12:17	Romans 12:15
Romans 12:14	Romans 12:18
Romans 13:8	Philippians 4:6
Hebrews 13:2	Hebrews 13:5
	Romans 12:19

Jesus knew His Scriptures. He was even able to teach the scribes in the temple when He was twelve years old.

Family Scripture study can help us be more like Jesus.

Why not start your family study with the Christmas story. Then try these other ideas.

DISCUSS: Go over the "findings" from the Scripture together. Repeat the instruction after you've written it.

READ TOGETHER: Each day for the next three weeks, read one of the Bible references together. Then agree to practice the instruction given—in your home and outside.

PRAY TOGETHER: Thank God for His Word which gives direction to Christians for living. Pray for enlightenment for your family as they study the Bible together to understand the "plan."

You are cordially invited

to attend the _____
(class name or teacher or director)

production of
"NIGHT OF NIGHTS"

A   Christmas   Musical

to be given on

_____   _____
(day, date)   (time)

at

_____
(location)

PLEASE COME!

Sincerely,

_____

NIGHT OF NIGHTS

Thanks for coming!

PROGRAM (insert)

NIGHT OF NIGHTS
—the players—

Narrator #1 _____

Narrator #2 _____

Angel Gabriel _____

Mary _____

Joseph _____

Innkeeper _____

Shepherds _____

Shepherd boy _____

Herald angel _____

Three wise men _____

Palace guards _____

King Herod _____

Palace servants _____

Chief Priest _____

Scribe _____

—behind the scenes—

Director _____

Asst. director _____

Costumes _____

Make-up _____

Scenery _____

Props _____

Programs _____

Invitations _____

Lighting _____

Sound _____

Stage crew _____

—Special thanks to all who made this production possible

COSTUMES & PROPS FOR "NIGHT OF NIGHTS"

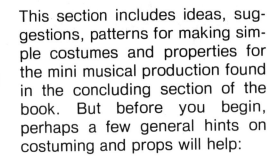

This section includes ideas, suggestions, patterns for making simple costumes and properties for the mini musical production found in the concluding section of the book. But before you begin, perhaps a few general hints on costuming and props will help:

1. Keep it simple. If the costumes become too elaborate and the scenery and props too complicated, it will detract from the overall beauty of the Christmas story, which should never be lost.

2. Keep costs down. Use what you have on hand or ask for donations before you BUY anything!

3. USE YOUR IMAGINATION! The best source of ideas is right in your own head and the children's heads! Put your heads together, look around, and you'll be amazed at the great costume and scenery ideas you will develop.

OUTFITTING A SHEPHERD

Let's dress up like shepherds!

First we need a shepherd's staff . . .

Here's how to make a simple one: Get an old broomstick or mop handle or piece of dowling, OR even one or two cardboard tubings from gift-wrap paper can be taped together. From cardboard, cut out two headpieces (suggested pattern on p.123) to form a hook at the top of your staff.

Place the hook piece on both sides of the top of your staff. Staple or glue the headpiece cut-outs together, making sure the staff is inserted at the bottom and secure.

Now paint the whole staff a brown color with poster or spray paint.

broomstick   **tubing**   staple or glue head- piece   **paint staff brown**

Now we need a headdress for those hot days and cold nights.

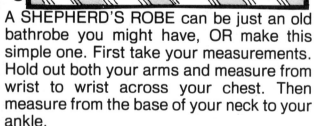

20"

20"   20"

head measurement plus 12"

6-8"

Take an old sheet and cut a triangle with sides that are 20 inches in length. Measure your head around your forehead. Take a contrasting piece of fabric (print or solid) that measures at least 12 inches longer than your head measurement. Make it about 6 to 8 inches wide. Roll the fabric into a rope. Place the white, triangular cloth on top of your head with one of the points hanging down the back of your neck. Take the rolled fabric, tie around your forehead to secure the white drape, and tuck in the tied ends.

A SHEPHERD'S ROBE can be just an old bathrobe you might have, OR make this simple one. First take your measurements. Hold out both your arms and measure from wrist to wrist across your chest. Then measure from the base of your neck to your ankle.

Also measure from your wrist to your underarm.

Now cut out your fabric according to the diagram at the right. Cut two and sew the seams as marked.

Measure your waist, add at least 24 inches, and cut another contrasting piece of fabric from the one you used on your headdress. Roll it and tie it around your waist.

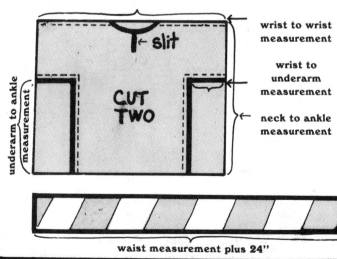

← slit

CUT TWO

underarm to ankle measurement

wrist to wrist measurement

wrist to underarm measurement

neck to ankle measurement

waist measurement plus 24"

SHEPHERD STAFF:
HEADPIECE PATTERN

CUT TWO

crown
patterns
see pp. 77, 78

CLOTHES FIT FOR A KING

Using the basic robe pattern for the shepherd, a king's costume can be made for either King Herod or the three wise men. Fancier or more colorful fabric could suggest a more costlier garment. Gold braid trim or pieces of old costume jewelry could be glued or sewn on to the fabric.

For King Herod, a simple cape can be added by sewing a two-inch hem at the end of rectangular piece of fabric and running a heavy piece of yarn or cord through the end to draw up and tie around the neck.

A jeweled scepter could also add to his regal appearance by gluing a styrofoam ball to the end of a piece of dowling (or the empty cylinder from a roll of gift wrap would do just as well). The entire scepter could be covered with aluminum foil and decorated with sequins, pieces of old costume jewelry, or even painted bottle caps. Be imaginative!

**Special hint: Red, purple, and royal blue are always very regal-looking colors to use.

sandals
see p. 127

DESIGNER DUDS

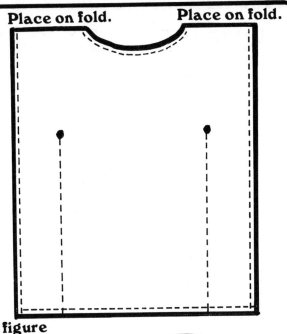

Place on fold.　　**Place on fold.**

figure
1

This is an alternative idea for making a simple robe pattern that may be used for Mary, Joseph, angels, OR even the shepherds, wise men and King Herod if colored fabric is unavailable. This is also less expensive.

Materials needed:
single sheets that can be dyed
one striped sheet for Joseph
light blue dye for Mary's costume
dark blue, green, brown dye for other costumes
pale yellow for the angels' costumes (or leave white)
cord
tinsel for halos/coat hangers

figure
2

Cut the sheets in half lengthwise. Fold in half. The piece will then measure about 3' 9'' long by 3' wide. Dye pieces for the specific characters. Cut a hole for the head. Stitch up to about 8 inches from the top to make sleeves. Hem where necessary. (See figure 1.) Belt the costumes for the boys with the cord.

Cut a long rectangle for Mary to drape over her head. It should hang down below her knees. The headpieces for the boys should be smaller rectangles that reach just to their shoulders. Tie cords around the heads. (See figure 2.)

Optional:
Halos for angels can be made by bending heavy wire or old coat hangers into the desired shapes. (See figure 3.) The hoop at the top of the halo can be covered with tinsel garland.

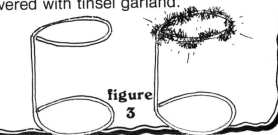

figure
3

WHAT WILL THE WISE MEN WEAR?

For wise men costumes, you can use the basic ideas suggested for the robes for the shepherds, King Herod and/or the Mary and Joseph. Make sure these three kings look regal and not just like three more shepherds without staffs.

The gifts the wise men bring to Baby Jesus can be made from shoe boxes, oatmeal boxes, fancy-shaped bottles covered with aluminum foil or foil gift wrap. Decorate them by gluing on sequins, colored yarn twisted into a pattern or design, and pieces of old costume jewelry.

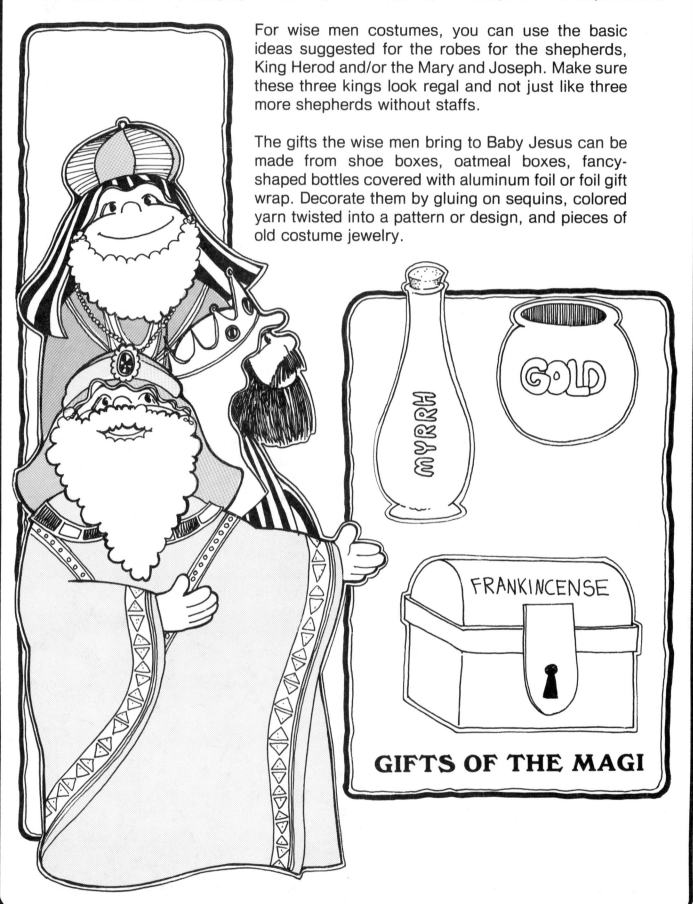

GIFTS OF THE MAGI

SANDAL CRAFT

1. Cut a foot pattern from cardboard.
2. Punch holes for lacing.
3. Place your foot on the cardboard.
4. Use knitting yarn and begin lacing in crisscross fashion from toes upward to knee.
5. Tie in bow at the top of calf.

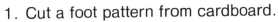

OPTIONAL PROPS

Other useful properties that can easily be added to your production without much time or expense will add to the overall effect. Use your imagination.

A shepherd's bedroll can be made from an old sheet stuffed with pillows or old clothes and tied with twine.

A fire can be made with the overhead projector technique used on page 128 and the pattern below.

The narrator(s) and the members of the chorus in the play do not have to be costumed. But they, along with small children who want to participate but who may not be able to remember lines, could be outfitted with large cardboard stars, painted, glittered and hung around their necks. They'll feel more like part of the production, too.

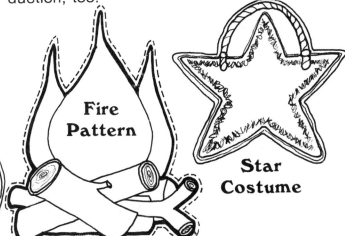

Fire Pattern

Star Costume

Shepherd's Bedroll

STAND-UP SCENERY

FOR THE SHEPHERD SCENE:

Enlarge these lambs to your specific needs by using an overhead projector. Trace the patterns on some clear transparency material and then place it on your projector. Now you are ready to make your stand-up lambs as large or as small as you desire.

You can project the lamb image onto butcher paper, cut out the figure, paste to cardboard and paint, OR you can project the image directly onto your cardboard, wood or whatever material you are using.

... AND MORE STAND-UP SCENERY

Enlarge these objects to suit your needs using the directions on the previous page.

WITHIN A LOWLY STABLE: A SIMPLIFIED
INN AND MANGER SCENE

Materials:
1 refrigerator box
1 piece of heavy cardboard, size 22'' x 28''
2 pieces of heavy cardboard, size 14'' x 22''
poster paint (white, brown, and yellow)
masking tape
a sharp knife

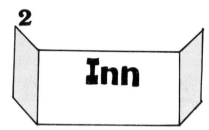

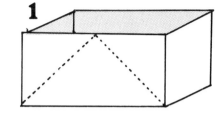

DIRECTIONS FOR MAKING THE STABLE:

Set the refrigerator box on its side. Cut the top, bottom and front from the refrigerator box. Cut a triangle from the front piece of the box. The base of the triangle should measure about 56 inches. (See figure 1.) Paint a yellow star on the front of the triangle.

On the back of the box, paint the word "INN" in large white letters on the top of the middle panel. (See figure 2.)

Paint the box brown. Cut slits on the bottom of the triangle about 5 inches deep and about 6 inches from each bottom point. (See figure 3.)

Cut corresponding slits 5 inches deep about 6 inches from the top edge on each side of the box. (See figure 4.) The side panels should stand out so they are open more than 90 degrees from the back panel. Fit the triangle slits into the slits in the base. This should brace the structure so it can be moved. (See figure 5.)

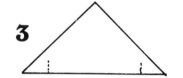

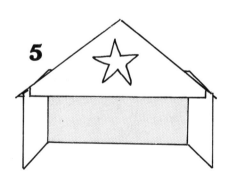

DIRECTIONS FOR MAKING THE MANGER:

Fold the 22'' x 28'' piece of cardboard in half by running a scissor blade straight across the cardboard to score it. (See figure 6.)

Fold the two smaller pieces of cardboard in half for the base. Cut away a triangle 2 inches wide by 6 inches deep. (See figure 7.)

Set the larger piece of cardboard into the triangle spaces. Tape together and paint. (See figure 8.)

A small doll can be placed in the finished manger.

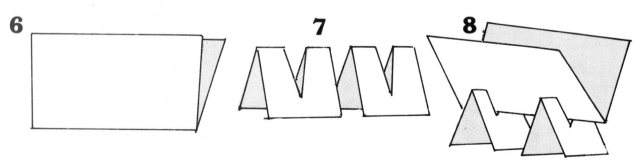

NIGHT OF NIGHTS

A Musical Drama for Christmas

—Cast of Characters—

Narrator #1	Three wise men
Narrator #2	Palace guards
Angel Gabriel	King Herod
Mary	Palace servants
Joseph	Chief Priest
Innkeeper	Scribe
Shepherds	Chorus
Shepherd boy	Host of angels
Herald angel	Townspeople

Setting: Palestine during the reign of Herod the Great. Caesar Augustus rules from Rome. The story begins in Nazareth of Galilee, then continues in Bethlehem and Jerusalem.

ACT I Scene 1

(A humble home in Nazareth—Mary is asleep on bedding on the floor near an open window; chorus is softly oohing ''Silent Night'' as curtain opens; Narrator #1 enters.)

NARRATOR #1   Long, long ago in a city of Galilee called Nazareth lived a beautiful maiden named Mary. She was betrothed to a righteous man by the name of Joseph. One night, Mary had a marvelous visit from a heavenly messenger. (Exits, oohing stops.)

GABRIEL: (enters with light through the window) Hail, Mary!

Shining Star Publications, Copyright © 1985. A division of Good Apple, Inc.

MARY:	(awakens, shows fear, gasps) Who are you? What do you want of me?
GABRIEL:	Fear not, Mary. You are most blessed among all the women on earth. You have found favor with God.
MARY:	With God? Are you a messenger from God?
GABRIEL:	I am the angel Gabriel, sent to bring you great news. You shall soon conceive and have a Son. His name shall be Jesus, and He will be called The Son of the Highest.
MARY:	But how can this be? My marriage to Joseph has not yet taken place, and we will not be . . .
GABRIEL:	By the power of God you shall bear a Son, and He shall be the Son of God.
MARY:	Who am I to be so chosen of the Lord? Can this be possible?
GABRIEL:	Behold, Mary. Your cousin Elisabeth has conceived a son in her old age. With God, nothing is impossible.
MARY:	Behold, I am the handmaid of the Lord. As you have spoken, so shall it be. With God all things are possible.
GABRIEL:	God be with you, Mary. You shall be blessed for your faith. (exits)
MARY:	Am I dreaming? Was that truly an angel of the Lord? I am to be the mother of the Son of God, the Holy One of Israel. Praise be to God! And my cousin Elisabeth! She is to be blessed with a child as well! I must visit her! And I must tell Joseph . . . . Joseph, dear Joseph, will he understand? Will he believe? I will leave it in God's hands. My beloved Joseph will not fail me. (kneeling) Glory to God! Praises to His most holy name! I am truly blessed! (curtain; chorus begins humming ''Silent Night'')

ACT I Scene 2

(Another humble home—Joseph prays at bedside; chorus oohs one verse of ''Who Was This Man Joseph?'' page 13; narrator #2 enters.)

NARRATOR #2:	The angel Gabriel was a busy messenger these days. He had foretold the birth of John the Baptist to Zacharias and Elisabeth and the birth of the Savior to Mary. And now another soul was in need of news from heaven.

JOSEPH:	(praying) Dear Lord. Help me. My beloved Mary is with child. How can this be? She says that this is from God. I want to believe, but my heart is heavy with grief. Help me, oh God! Help me to know what to do! (covers face with hands, drops to bed, falls asleep; chorus sings 1st verse of ''Who Was This Man Joseph?'')
GABRIEL:	(enters from window basked in light; speaks to Joseph as he dreams) Fear not, Joseph. Take Mary as your wife. She has been chosen to be the mother of God's only begotten Son. His name shall be called Jesus, and you, Joseph, shall be His guardian. Sleep well, Joseph; trust in the Lord. (exits)
JOSEPH:	(waking from sleep) What dream was this? Was that truly an angel of the Lord? (on knees) Praise be to God! He has answered my prayers! Yes, I shall take Mary as my wife. And she shall bear the Holy Child, the Son of the Most High. His name shall be Jesus. I am truly blessed among men!

ACT I Scene 3

(Just outside city—Joseph secures provisions as Mary sits on a donkey; chorus oohs ''A Long, Dark Road,'' page 6; narrators enter)

NARRATOR #1:	So Joseph took Mary as his wife, just as the Lord had directed. The time drew near when Mary would soon give birth to the Baby who would be called Jesus. This was no time to be making long journeys.
NARRATOR #2:	But Caesar Augustus had decreed that all the world should be taxed. Every man was to go to the city of his birth, and Joseph had to journey to Bethlehem. Joseph was concerned the trip might be hard on his beloved Mary, now heavy with child.
JOSEPH:	Mary, I'm not sure it's wise for you to travel. What if the baby comes too soon? What if we cannot find a comfortable place for you in Bethlehem?
MARY:	We have no choice, Joseph. I must go with you. Do not worry, my husband. God will provide for us. Have faith. (Joseph nods, begins leading donkey away.)
CHORUS:	(sings 1st verse of ''A Long, Dark Road,'' page 6; then oohs as Mary and Joseph continue walking back and forth as if on a long journey; curtain)

ACT II Scene 1

(Bethlehem—Joseph and Mary go from inn to inn knocking on doors, being turned away; chorus sings ''O Little Town of Bethlehem''; townspeople walk about the streets.)

NARRATOR #1:	So on and on went Joseph and Mary until finally they arrived in Bethlehem. And what a noisy, crowded place it was. Joseph did not expect this.
JOSEPH:	(Knocks at inn door; innkeeper opens door.) Please, sir. We have looked everywhere. My wife's time is very near. Don't you have even a small room where we could . . .
INNKEEPER:	No! There is no room! There is no room anywhere in Bethlehem! Are you blind, man? Look around you! Begone! (slams door)
JOSEPH:	(sadly bows head, turns back toward Mary)
INNKEEPER:	(opens door) Wait! There's a stable around back. You'd have to share it with the animals. But it's better than the streets. It's clean, and there's fresh hay to lie on. You're welcome to it.
JOSEPH:	Thank you, sir. You're very kind.
INNKEEPER:	I'm sorry. It's the best I can do. (closes door)
JOSEPH:	Thank you. (turns to Mary) How I wish . . .
MARY:	The stable will be fine, Joseph. Let's get settled. This baby is not going to wait much longer. (Joseph begins helping Mary around to the stable.)
CHORUS:	(sings both verses of ''I Wonder,'' page 9)
NARRATOR #2:	(Stage darkens, spotlight on narrator only.) And so, on that night of nights, in a quiet stable in crowded little Bethlehem, was born the Christ Child, the Savior of the world. It was a humble beginning for the Prince of Peace; not in a castle or a palace, but within a lowly stable did the earth receive God's greatest gift.
CHORUS:	(sings all verses of ''Within a Lowly Stable,'' page 56; continues oohing melody while narrator finishes; spotlight on Mary, Joseph and Baby Jesus in manger)
NARRATOR #1:	But this night of nights was far from over. There would be witnesses to the glorious birth that all the world would remember in verse and Scripture for all time. (curtain)

ACT II Scene 2

(Outside Bethlehem in a shepherd's field—this scene could take place in front of the curtain if changing sets is too difficult; shepherds watching flocks)

CHORUS:	(sings 1 verse of "The First Noel" as curtain opens; oohs as narrators enter)
NARRATOR #2:	Not far from that stable in Bethlehem, some humble shepherds were about to have an experience that would live in their hearts and the hearts of all men forever.
SHEPHERD #1:	My, but it's quiet tonight. I can hardly stay awake.
SHEPHERD #2:	I'll bet it's not quiet in town tonight. Did you see the crowds of people pouring in to be counted for that taxation Rome is demanding?
SHEPHERD #3:	Please let's not talk of Rome or Caesar. You'll spoil a perfectly beautiful evening. (yawns)
SHEPHERD BOY:	Why don't all of you go to sleep for a while. I'll watch the sheep. Nothing will happen.
SHEPHERD #1:	Thank you, son. Let's take him up on it, men. (Three shepherds lay down and begin to sleep.)
CHORUS:	(sings both verses of "The Shepherds' Story," page 32)

(Stage becomes filled with light as herald angel enters the scene; shepherd boy shrinks in fear.)

SHEPHERD BOY:	Father, Father!
SHEPHERD #1:	What is it, boy? (All three shepherds awaken; they see the angel and are afraid.)
HERALD ANGEL:	Fear not. Behold, I bring you good tidings of great joy, which shall be to all people. For unto you is born this day in the city of David, a Savior, which is Christ the Lord.
SHEPHERD #2:	(kneeling) Christ, the Lord? Our promised Messiah?
SHEPHERD #3:	How shall we know Him?
HERALD ANGEL:	This shall be a sign unto you; you shall find Baby Jesus wrapped in swaddling clothes, lying in a manger.
HOST OF ANGELS:	(enter singing "Let the Bells Ring Out," page 21; shepherds and chorus join in on 2nd verse.)
SHEPHERD #1:	Glory to God! Christ the Lord is born this night and God has sent His angels to tell us, **to tell us,** the great news! (Optional: ensemble sings 1 verse of "Hark the Herald Angels Sing.")

SHEPHERD BOY:	Can we go and see Him, Father? The angel said He was lying in a manger. Do you think we can find Him?
SHEPHERD #1:	Yes, son. Yes. We must find the Christ Child so that we might worship Him. Come, let us go to Bethlehem. God will help us find our Lord.
SHEPHERD #2:	Look, there in the sky. That star is growing brighter.
SHEPHERD #3:	I see it!
SHEPHERD BOY:	Let's follow it! It will show us where the Christ Child is! (Shepherds slowly exit.)
CHORUS:	(sings 2nd verse of "A Long, Dark Road," page 6, as shepherds exit)
NARRATOR #1:	God has brought the first news of Christ's birth not to mighty kings or rulers, but to humble shepherds. What better way to learn that God's greatest gift of love was not given to a few, but to all people. (Curtain falls as chorus oohs "A Long, Dark Road.")

ACT II Scene 3

(The stable in Bethlehem—Mary and Joseph have Baby Jesus; shepherds approach.)

CHORUS:	(sings "In a Manger," page 55)
SHEPHERD BOY:	He is here, Father. I know it! See the way the light shines from the stable?
SHEPHERD #1:	Shhh, my son! This is a holy place. Let us enter reverently.
SHEPHERD #2:	(to Joseph) We have come to worship the Christ Child. May we enter?
JOSEPH:	(looks at Mary; Mary nods) Yes, come in. How did you know He was here?
SHEPHERD #2:	An angel of the Lord appeared to us in the field while we watched our flocks.
SHEPHERD BOY:	I have brought Him my best lamb. It is a gift.
MARY:	Thank you.
SHEPHERD BOY:	What's His name?
MARY:	His name is Jesus.

SHEPHERD BOY:	Little Lord Jesus, happy birthday!
MARY:	(smiling) Yes, it is a happy, happy birthday. Not just for Baby Jesus, but for the whole earth.
SHEPHERD #1:	That is what the angel said, that the good news would bring joy to all people.
SHEPHERD #2:	And then the angels sang of peace and good will for all.
SHEPHERD #3:	Perhaps at last we will be rid of this cursed Roman rule!
JOSEPH:	I wonder if that's the kind of peace they meant.
MARY:	Speaking of peace, did you ever see a more peaceful baby?
SHEPHERD BOY:	He's asleep! Look, Father.
CHORUS:	(and shepherds sing ''Away in a Manger''; ooh the melody as narrator finishes scene)
NARRATOR #2:	This truly was a night of nights. There was something special in the air. Perhaps many more than any of us know felt the specialness of that first Christmas night. But there would be others who would yet find their way into the first Christmas story, who would be led by God to the Christ Child, little Lord Jesus. (curtain)

ACT III Scene 1

(Road outside Jerusalem—three wise men enter in front of curtain; narrator stands at one side of stage as chorus oohs ''A Long, Dark Road, '' page 6.)

CHORUS:	(sings final verse of ''A Long, Dark Road'')
NARRATOR #1:	While all these events were taking place in Bethlehem, another part of the Christmas story was unfolding in Jerusalem. Wise men from the East had seen a star and had followed it to Judea searching for the child prophesied to become King of the Jews.
WISE MAN #1:	We must be close to our journey's end. There is Jerusalem—the Holy City of the Jews. Surely we will find the Holy Child here.
WISE MAN #2:	I am told that Herod is the king who reigns now. Let us go to his palace and seek the whereabouts of this newborn King. Surely he will know.

WISE MAN #3:	I hope so. This has been a long and wearisome journey. Let us go. (slowly travel across stage)
CHORUS:	(sings 1st verse of "Wise Men, Brave Men," page 66)

ACT III Scene 2

(Palace of King Herod—Herod sits on throne attended by servants; guards enter.)

GUARD #1:	(salutes, arm to chest) Your Majesty. We have found three travelers, kings from the East, just outside the city. They wish an audience with you.
GUARD #2:	They claim you can help them in their quest.
HEROD:	Their quest for what?
GUARD #1:	The King of the Jews.
HEROD:	I am King of the Jews. How can I help them find me? They've already done that! Oh, show them in.
GUARD #2:	Yes, Your Majesty! (Both salute, exit.)
HEROD:	Fetch me the Chief Priest and scribe. I think I'm going to need some help with these kings.
SERVANT:	(bowing) Yes, Your Majesty. (exits)
GUARD #1:	(re-enters with wise men) Here are the men, Your Majesty.
HEROD:	Thank you, guard. That is all. (Guards exit.) Now, gentlemen, what is this about the King of the Jews? You see before you just that.
WISE MAN #3:	No, mighty Herod. The King we seek has been foretold for centuries. He shall deliver your people. He will rule the world.
WISE MAN #1:	Yes. We were told in a dream we should seek the Holy Child. This is the time of His birth.
WISE MAN #2:	We have seen His star in the East and have come to worship Him.

(Re-enter servant with Chief Priest and scribe.)

HEROD:	Oh good. Here are my . . . uh . . . religious advisors. They will help me answer your questions. What do we know of this promised Messiah? I've heard the Jews speak of this Christ. When and where is He supposed to be born?

CHIEF PRIEST: The Scriptures tell us He will be born in Bethlehem of Judea. It was written by the Prophet that out of Bethlehem shall come a governor who will rule my people Israel.

SCRIBE: Exactly when He is to be born is difficult to tell.

HEROD: Very well. Thank you. That is all.

SCRIBE: Why do you ask, mighty Herod? Have these men . . .

HEROD: I said, that is all. I'll call you if I need any more . . . advice. (Chief Priest and scribe leave; Herod turns to the three wise men.) Please, good men, go to Bethlehem. Find this newborn King, the Christ Child, and when you have found Him, bring me word that I might come and worship Him as well.

WISE MAN #1: Thank you, King Herod. You have helped us greatly.

WISE MAN #2: We shall do as you ask.

WISE MAN #3: Let us go to Bethlehem at once. (All exit.)

HEROD: Yes, at once, and when you find Him, I'll make sure this newborn King is never burdened with the responsibility of being a deliverer to His people.

CHORUS: (repeats 1st verse of ''Wise Men, Brave Men,'' page 66, as curtain closes on palace scene)

ACT III Scene 3

(Optional setting: wise men may join shepherds, Mary and Joseph in traditional setting at stable, OR, if set design permits, curtain will open on interior of humble home where wise men are presenting gifts to the Christ Child; see Matthew 2:11.)

CHORUS: (as curtain re-opens, sings 2nd verse of ''Wise Men, Brave Men,'' page 66)

NARRATOR #2: So the wise men did find Baby Jesus in Bethlehem, and when they had found Him, they worshipped Him and opened their treasures of gold and frankincense and myrrh.

WISE MAN #1: Farewell, Joseph. Thank you for letting us present this Holy Child with our gifts we have brought from afar.

WISE MAN #2: Yes, thank you. Our quest is now ended. We have seen the child we have sought for so long.

JOSEPH: Must you go?

WISE MAN #3:   Yes, we have news to spread. We must be on our way.

MARY: Farewell, good men, and thank you.

(The wise men travel back and forth across the stage as if traveling while narrator #1 speaks; then they lie down to sleep.)

NARRATOR #1:   But now that the kings from the East had found the Holy One they had been seeking, they felt a bit uneasy about returning to Herod with their news.

CHORUS: (sings final verse of ''Wise Men, Brave Men,'' page 66; while singing, wise men rise and leave stage.)

NARRATOR #2:   Because they had been forewarned, the three wise men returned to their own country another way avoiding Jerusalem and King Herod.

NARRATOR #1:   Now that the wondrous birth had been heralded to both the humble and noble alike, Mary and Joseph had much to ponder in their hearts concerning this night of nights.

MARY: (steps forward with Christ Child in arms) Oh, Joseph. What a wonder, what a miracle this child is. Truly God has blessed us both beyond our wildest dreams.

JOSEPH: (steps to her side) Little Lord Jesus, the only begotten Son of God, come to Earth to save all people. Angels, shepherds, wise men all have come to praise and to worship this Holy Child. (As Joseph names shepherds, angels, wise men, they step onto stage in background.) The world will not soon forget this wondrous night, this HOLY NIGHT, THIS NIGHT OF NIGHTS!

CHORUS: (and ensemble sing verses of ''Silent Night''; audience may be invited to join in.)

CURTAIN

PRODUCTION TIPS FOR "NIGHT OF NIGHTS"

1. Practice **SINGING ONLY** for your first rehearsals. The entire cast should learn all the verses to all the songs. Assign solo parts where you feel your cast members have the ability and where it is appropriate (parts of "Wise Men, Brave Men," "Within a Lowly Stable," "Let the Bells Ring Out").

2. If accompaniment is not available, practice with **TAPED MUSIC.**

3. Practice the speaking parts in small groups **OFFSTAGE.** Have several rehearsals before going to the stage.

4. When first going to the stage to block the action, **SPEAKING AND SINGING PARTS SHOULD ALREADY BE MEMORIZED.** This will save a lot of time once you start practicing on stage.

5. **CASTING:** The main cast is designed for a single class presentation. However, for multi-class presentations or for very large groups, small children could be dressed as **STARS, LAMBS, ADDITIONAL ANGELS,** and assigned solo parts in the songs using a few measures for each child or group of children.

6. **SET DESIGN:** If flats are used, make them reversible so that you can change the setting from home to stable, from outdoor to palace by just turning the scenery. **Also,** large cardboard boxes like refrigerator boxes or other appliance cartons make excellent scenery when painted. Use simple supports.

CERTIFICATE OF MERIT

is hereby awarded to

_____

for an outstanding performance
as

_____

in the Christmas Musical Drama
"NIGHT OF NIGHTS"

performed on _____
date

_____
teacher

THANK-YOU NOTE: Send to parents and friends who contributed in any way to making your Christmas production a success.

Directions: Duplicate as many thank-you notes as you'll need. Cut out each note, fold in half using the dotted lines as guides, and print your thank-you message on the inside. For a personal touch, have children deliver the thank-you notes.

THANK YOU

ANSWER KEY

MARY AND JOSEPH p. 5
Luke 2:1, 4

RIDDLE RACE p.26
Riddle #1 = Zacharias
Challenge Riddle = John the Baptist

CONNECT p. 43
A. BIG DIPPER
   (Ursa Major)
B. LITTLE DIPPER
   (Ursa Minor)
C. CASSIOPEIA
D. ORION
E. DRACO
F. TAURUS

HOW MANY STARS? p. 51
Answer: 43 overlapping stars

THE JESSE TREE p. 88
Adam & Eve, apple (Genesis 3:6)
Moses, tablets (Exodus 20:11)
David, harp (II Samual 22:1)
Jacob, ladder (Genesis 28:12)
Joseph, coat (Genesis 37:3)
Mary, lily (Luke 1:27)
Jesus, manger (Luke 2:7)

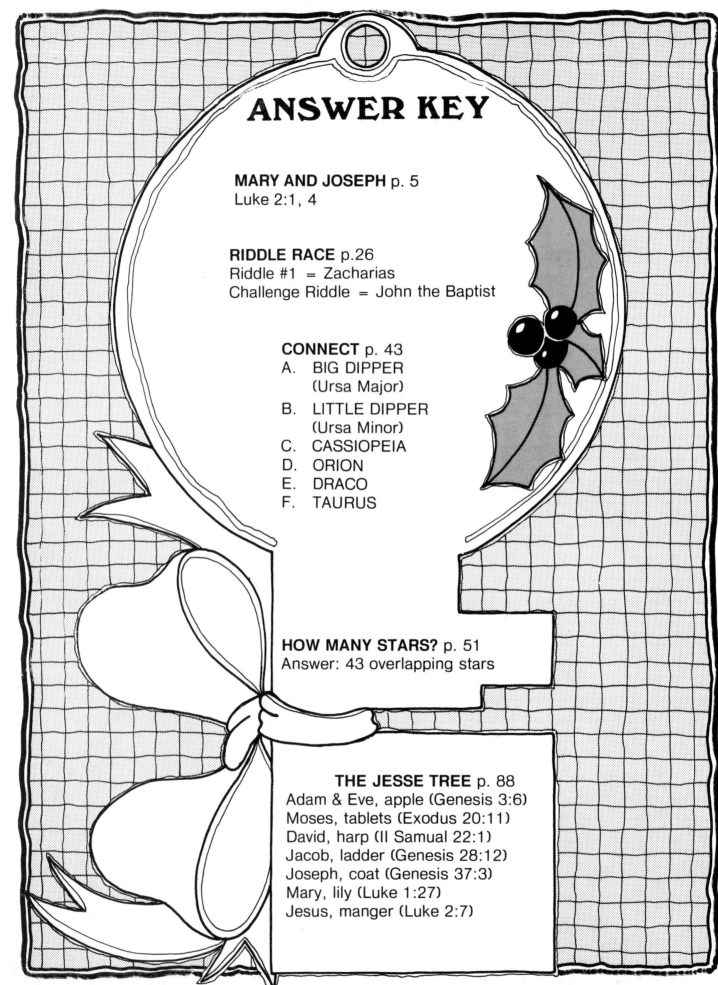